NEIGHBORHOODS AND COMMUNITIES

A firehouse is one of the special places found in every neighborhood. The firefighters help to keep us safe. Does a dog live in the firehouse in your neighborhood?

BARRY K. BEYER

JEAN CRAVEN

MARY A. McFARLAND

WALTER C. PARKER

MACMILLAN PUBLISHING COMPANY, NEW YORK
COLLIER MACMILLAN PUBLISHERS, LONDON

PROGRAM AUTHORS

Dr. Barry K. Beyer
Professor of Education and American Studies
George Mason University
Fairfax, Virginia

Jean Craven
Social Studies Coordinator
Albuquerque Public Schools
Albuquerque, New Mexico

Dr. Mary A. McFarland
Instructional Coordinator of Social Studies,
 K–12 and Director of Staff Development
Parkway School District
Chesterfield, Missouri

Dr. Walter C. Parker
Associate Professor, College of Education
University of Washington
Seattle, Washington

CONTENT CONSULTANTS

Reading
Dr. Virginia Arnold
Senior Author, *Connections* Reading Program
Richmond, Virginia

Economics
Dr. George Dawson
Professor of Economics
Empire State University
Bellmore, New York

Special Populations
Dr. Jeannette Fleischner
Professor of Education
Teachers College
Columbia University
New York, New York

Curriculum
John Sanford
Director of Curriculum
Acalanes Union High School District
Lafayette, California

Multicultural
Dr. Joe Trotter
Professor of History
Carnegie Mellon University
Pittsburgh, Pennsylvania

History
Dr. David Van Tassel
Founder of United States History Week
Professor of History
Case Western Reserve University
Cleveland, Ohio

Geography
Nancy Winter
Member of the Executive Board of the
 National Council for Geographic Education
Social Studies Teacher
Bedford, Massachusetts

International Education
Gary Yee
Principal
Hillcrest School
Oakland, California

GRADE-LEVEL CONSULTANTS

Monica Boylan Bonner
Elementary Teacher
Dr. Charles DeFuccio School P.S. 39
Jersey City, New Jersey

Nancy Garvey
Elementary Teacher
Griffin Memorial School
Litchfield, New Hampshire

LouWonne Kuhlmann
Second Grade Teacher
Schleswig Community School
Schleswig, Iowa

Nelda G. Liles
Reading Coordinator
Provencal Elementary School
Natchitoches, Louisiana

Ruby Polley
Elementary Teacher
Bentalou Elementary School #150
Columbia, Maryland

CONTRIBUTING WRITER

Loretta Kaim
Peekskill, New York

ACKNOWLEDGMENTS

The publisher gratefully acknowledges permission to reprint the following copyrighted material:
"Indian Stick Song" appears in MUSIC AND YOU: GRADE 3, Barbara Staton and Merrill Staton, Senior
Authors (New York: Macmillan, 1988). "You're a Grand Old Flag" appears in MUSIC AND YOU: GRADE 3,
Barbara Staton and Merrill Staton, Senior Authors (New York: Macmillan, 1988). "Rides" by Ilo Orleans
appeared originally in *Child Life,* 1953. Used by permission of Karen S. Solomon.

Macmillan Publishing Company
866 Third Avenue
New York, New York 10022
Collier Macmillan Canada, Inc.

Printed in the United States of America
ISBN 0-02-144020-4
9 8 7 6

CONTENTS

UNIT 4 Living on the Earth   108

UNIT 5 America Long Ago   140

Charts, Graphs, Diagrams, and Time Lines

Maps and Globes

USING YOUR TEXTBOOK

Your book has many pages that can help you use things in it.

The **Table of Contents** is at the front of your book. It can help you find the things that are in your book.

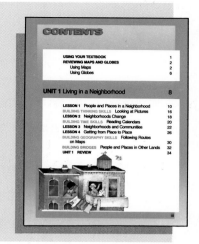

Reviewing **Maps and Globes** can help you use the maps and globes in your book.

The **Picture Glossary** tells you the meaning of each new word that you will learn. It also has a sentence and a picture for each new word.

The **Atlas** has some special maps. You can use the maps in the Atlas as you learn about new places.

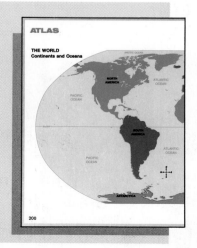

Using Maps

A **map** is a drawing of a place. Maps are flat. They show what places look like from above.

Maps can show many things. This is a special map called a floor plan. A floor plan shows the rooms in a place.

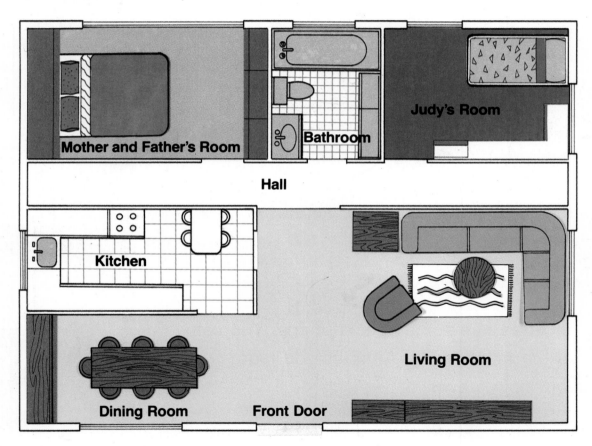

What kind of place does the floor plan show? home
What rooms can you see? What two rooms are next to the Kitchen?

2

Many maps have symbols. A symbol is
something that stands for something else.
Symbols on a map can be pictures, shapes, or
colors that stand for real things. To find out what
symbols on a map stand for, look at the map key.
A map key tells what each symbol means.

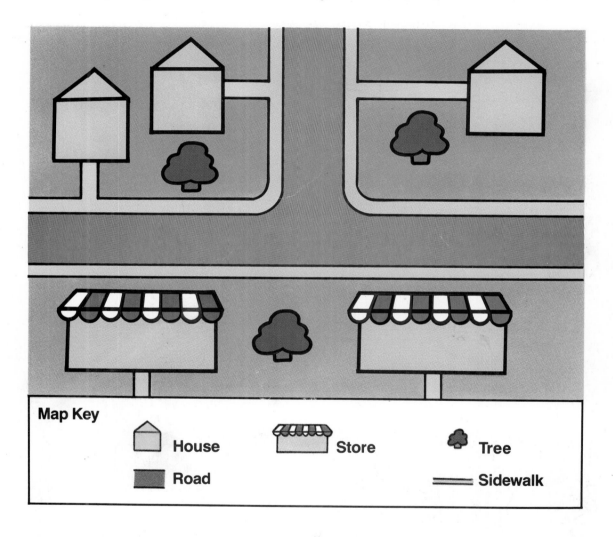

Find the map key on the map. What symbol
stands for a House? How many Stores are on the
map? What other things does the map show?

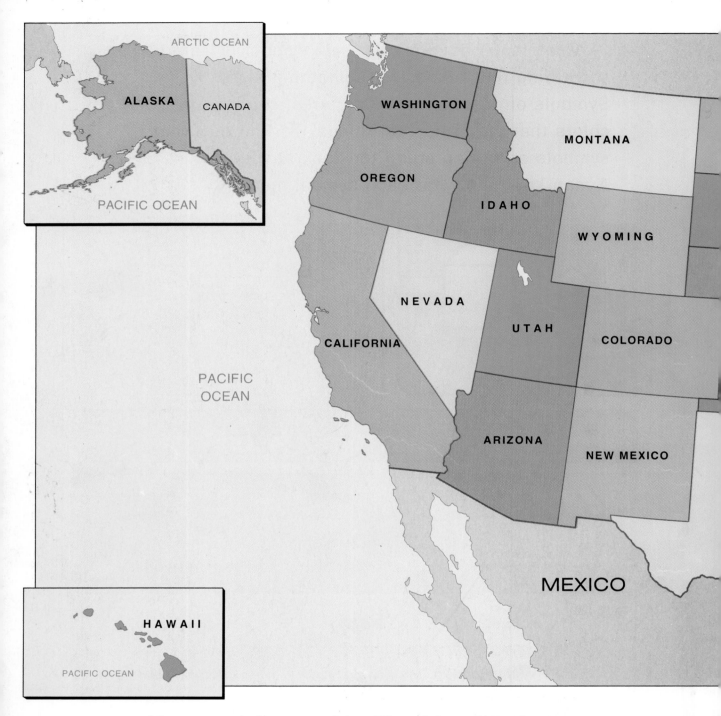

Most maps have a title. The title tells what
the map shows. What is the title of this map?

The United States is a country. A country is a
land and the people who live there. The people who
live in the United States are called Americans.

4

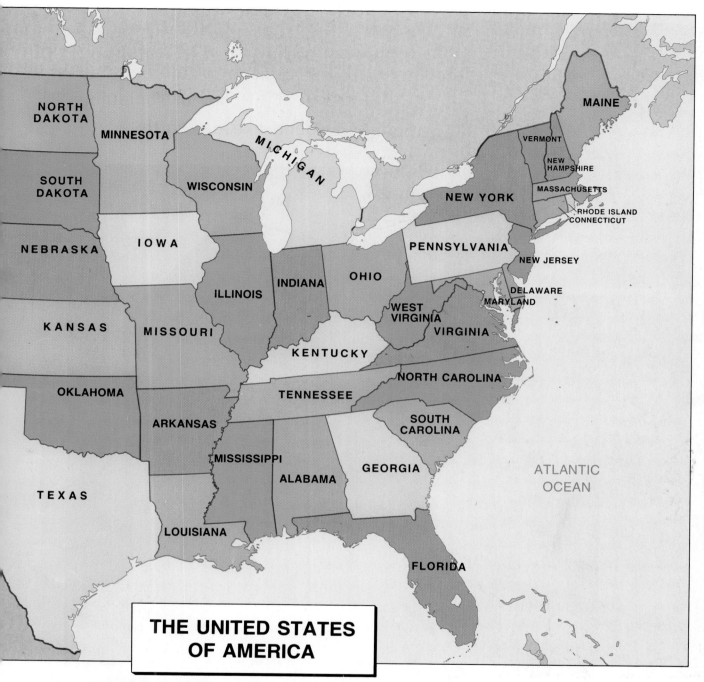

THE UNITED STATES OF AMERICA

The United States is made up of 50 states.
Each state has a name. Many maps show the names
of places, like states. They also show the names
of different bodies of water.

Name two things that maps can show.

Using Globes

A **globe** is a model of the earth.
A model is a small copy of something.
A globe is round like the earth.

North Pole

South Pole

A globe shows places on the earth. This side of the globe shows many countries. Find the United States on the globe.

There are four important **directions** on the earth. They are north, east, south, and west.

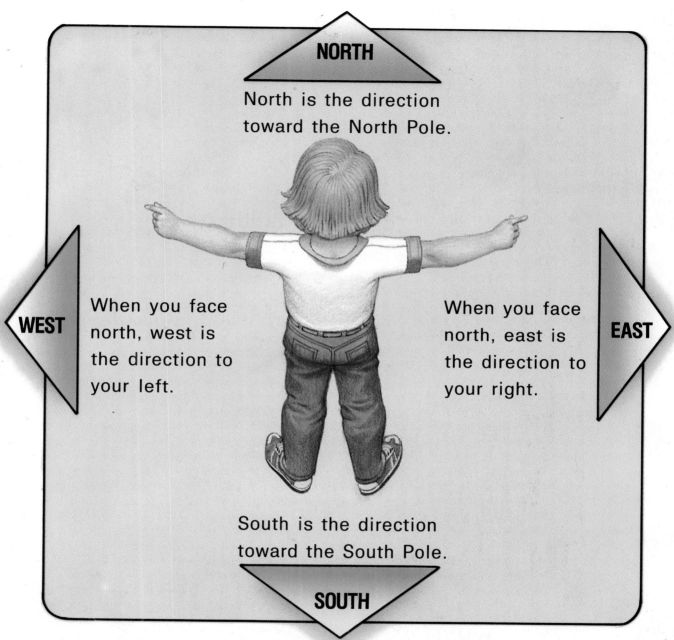

NORTH

North is the direction toward the North Pole.

WEST

When you face north, west is the direction to your left.

EAST

When you face north, east is the direction to your right.

South is the direction toward the South Pole.

SOUTH

Look at the globe on page 6. Find Canada. Canada is the country that is north of the United States. What country is south of the United States?

 How is a globe like the earth?

town

suburb

communities

city

transportation

8

Living in a Neighborhood

neighborhood

neighbors

People and Places in a Neighborhood

Mike has just moved into a house in a different **neighborhood**. A neighborhood is a place where people live, work, and play.

Ann lives in the house next to Mike's house. Ann is Mike's **neighbor**. Neighbors are people who live near one another in a neighborhood.

Every neighborhood has homes where people live. In the neighborhood where Mike used to live, the homes were close together.

In the neighborhood where Mike lives now, the homes are farther apart.

Mike's neighborhood also has places
where people can learn, play, get help,
and shop.

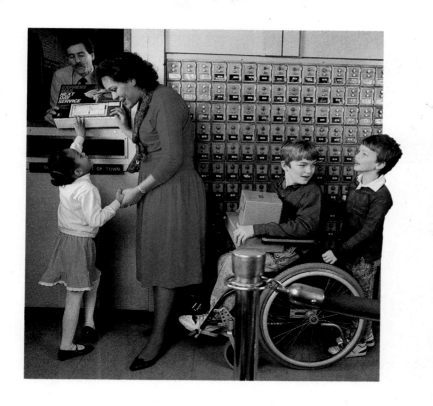

What can Mike and his neighbors
do at these places?

13

This picture shows a neighborhood like
Mike's neighborhood. It shows how this
neighborhood looks from an airplane. What
things can you see in this neighborhood?

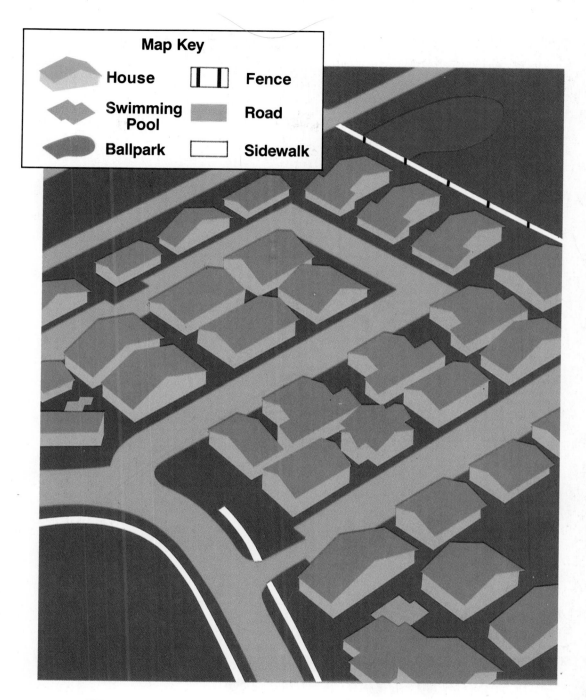

Map Key

House		Fence	
Swimming Pool		Road	
Ballpark		Sidewalk	

This map shows the neighborhood that is in the picture. What is in the picture that is not on the map?

What is a neighborhood?

What places might you find in a neighborhood?

Looking at Pictures

1. **LOOK** at the picture.

TELL what the people are doing.

Helping Yourself

One way to look at pictures is to:

■ **CHOOSE** what to look at it in the picture.

■ **LOOK** closely to see all you can about it.

■ **LOOK** at it closely from all sides.

■ **TELL** all you can about the thing you chose.

Do the four steps many times until you find out everything that you need to know.

2. The people in the picture are doing many things. Did you see the children playing ball? Did you see the people singing? What other things did you see people doing?

3. LOOK at the picture again.
TELL where the place is.

4. What steps could you use to look at pictures? What kinds of things do you look at?

Neighborhoods Change

The people who live in a neighborhood may change. People may move out of a neighborhood and people may move into a neighborhood. What are these people doing?

Places in a neighborhood may also change. How is this part of Mike's neighborhood changing?

These pictures show the same neighborhood. The top picture shows how the neighborhood looked many years ago. The bottom picture shows how the neighborhood looks today. In what ways has this neighborhood changed?

 What kinds of changes may take place in a neighborhood?

Reading Calendars

Calendars are special charts that show the months of the year. They show the number of days that are in each month. Calendars also show on which day of the week a certain date will fall.

October

Sunday	Monday	Tuesday	Wednesday	Thursday	Friday	Saturday
		1	2	3	4	5
6	7	8	9	10	11	12
13	14	15	16	17	18	19
20	21	22	23	24	25	26
27	28	29	30	31		

Use the calendar to answer the questions.

1. What month does the calendar show?
2. How many days are in the month?
3. On which day of the week is October 1?
4. On which day of the week is October 31?
5. What is the date of the third Wednesday of the month?

20

Calendars also help to remind us when we have to go places and do things. They help us to remember special days.

October						
Sunday	Monday	Tuesday	Wednesday	Thursday	Friday	Saturday
		1 ✗	2 ✗	3 ✗	4 ✗	5 ✗
6 ✗	7 ✗	8 ✗	9 ✗	10	11 moving day	12
13	14 first day at new school	15	16	17	18	19
20	21	22	23	24	25	26
27 Amy's Birthday Party	28	29	30	31		

Aaron circled a special day on his calendar. Each night, before he goes to sleep, Aaron crosses off the day that has just ended on his calendar.

Use Aaron's calendar to answer the questions.
1. What special day did Aaron circle?
2. On which day of the week does it fall?
3. How many days has Aaron crossed off?
4. What will Aaron do on October 14?
5. What will Aaron do on the last Sunday of the month?

Neighborhoods and Communities

Mike's neighborhood is part of a
community. Some communities have
many neighborhoods.

There are different kinds of communities.
One kind of community is a city. A city is a
very large community. Many people live
in a city. A city is made up of many
neighborhoods. This picture shows the
city of Memphis, Tennessee. Mike's
neighborhood is in the city of Memphis.

These places are in some of the neighborhoods that make up the city of Memphis. What kinds of places do you see in the city of Memphis?

Another kind of community is a **suburb**. A suburb is a community just outside of a city. Suburbs are often smaller than a city. Some people who live in a suburb work in the city nearby.

This picture shows a suburb of the city of Memphis. Mike's friend, Tim, lives in this suburb of Memphis.

Some people live in another kind of community called a town. A town is a small community with fewer people than a city or a suburb.

Some people live in a farm community. In a farm community many people live and work on farms. The farms may be very far apart. Mike visits his grandparents' farm each summer.

Is your community a city, a suburb, a town, or a farm community?

 Name four kinds of communities. Tell how they are different.

Getting from Place to Place

Mike can walk to most of the places in his neighborhood.

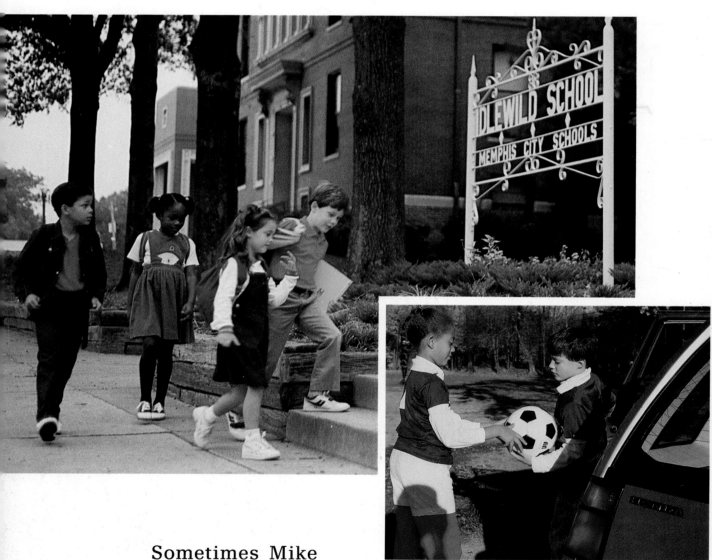

Sometimes Mike needs to use transportation to get to other places where he wants to go. Transportation is a way of moving people from place to place.

Many people live in one community, but may shop, work, go to school, or visit people in a different community. Transportation, like buses, can move people to places in other communities. Mike's mother takes the bus to her job.

Trains and subways are other kinds of transportation. Subways are special trains that run under the ground.

Some people may need to cross water
to get from place to place. They may need to
take a special kind of boat called a ferry.

Some people live very far away from
where they want to go. They may take an
airplane to get there. The city of Memphis
has a busy airport with many airplanes.

This poem tells about rides on different kinds of transportation. What rides have you taken? What rides would you like to take?

Rides

I ride on a bus.
I ride on a train.
I ride on a trolley.
I ride on a plane.
I ride on a ferry.
I ride in a car.
I ride on my skates—
But not very far.
But, best of all,
The ride I like
Is 'round the block
On my new bike.

by Ilo Orleans

Name two kinds of transportation.

Following Routes on Maps

Mrs. Marino, the school bus driver, follows a **route** to pick up children for school. A route is the way a person goes from one place to another. Mrs. Marino's school bus makes many stops along her route.

Mrs. Marino's School Bus Route

Stop 1 – Pick up John in front of his home on Pear Street.

Stop 2 – Pick up Martha on the corner of Wood Road and Apple Street.

Stop 3 – Pick up Andrew on the corner of Apple Street and Rocky Road.

Stop 4 – Pick up Maggie and Lewis on the corner of Wood Road and Plum Street.

Stop 5 – Drop off children in front of the school on Cherry Street.

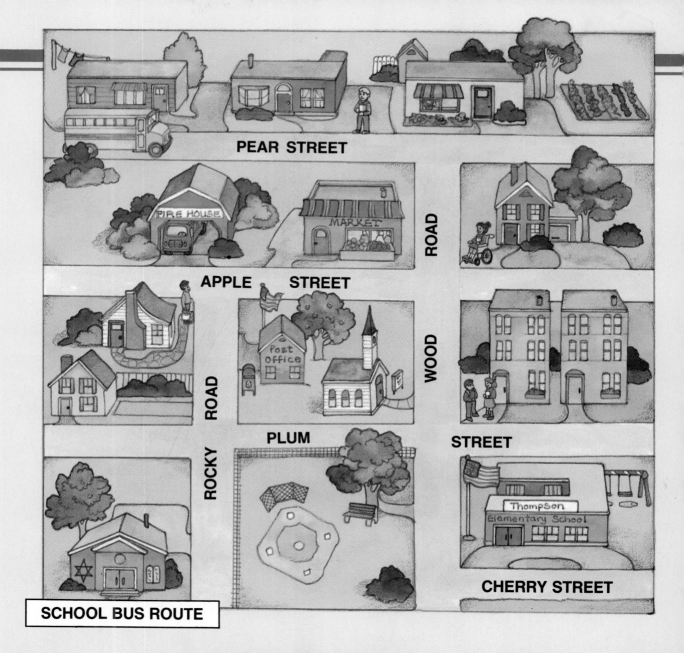

PEAR STREET

FIRE HOUSE

MARKET

ROAD

APPLE STREET

ROAD

Post Office

WOOD

ROCKY ROAD

PLUM

STREET

Thompson Elementary School

SCHOOL BUS ROUTE

CHERRY STREET

Find each stop that Mrs. Marino's school bus makes on the map. Move your finger on the map to show the route that Mrs. Marino's school bus follows. What is the first street that Mrs. Marino drives on?

You can use more than one route to go somewhere. Find two ways to go from Andrew's house to school.

People and Places in Other Lands

Rosa and her family live in a country called Mexico. They live in a neighborhood in a large city called Mexico City.

There are many places in Rosa's neighborhood. There is a firehouse and a school. There are many street markets, too. Rosa and her family do most of their shopping at these street markets.

Rosa and her family
like to go to Mexico City's
biggest park. They ride
there on the subway called the Metro.
The Metro is just one of the changes that
has taken place in Rosa's neighborhood
over the years.

Name three places in Rosa's neighborhood.
What change has taken place in Rosa's
neighborhood?

Words You Learned

Tell if each sentence is true or false.

1. All <u>neighborhoods</u> have homes.
2. People who live near one another in a neighborhood are <u>neighbors</u>.
3. A <u>community</u> is part of a neighborhood.
4. A <u>city</u> is a small community.
5. Some people who live in a <u>suburb</u> work in the city nearby.
6. A <u>town</u> is a small community with fewer people than a city or a suburb.
7. Buses are one kind of <u>transportation</u>.

Ideas You Learned

1. Name a place in a neighborhood that everyone can use.
2. How can homes in a neighborhood be different?
3. Name two ways a neighborhood can change.
4. Tell how a city and a town are alike. Tell how they are different.
5. Tell why people may need to use transportation.

Building Skills

1. Reviewing Looking at Pictures

LOOK at the picture.

a. TELL all you can see about the people.

b. TELL all you can see about the places.

2. Reviewing Following Routes on Maps

Use the map below to answer the questions.

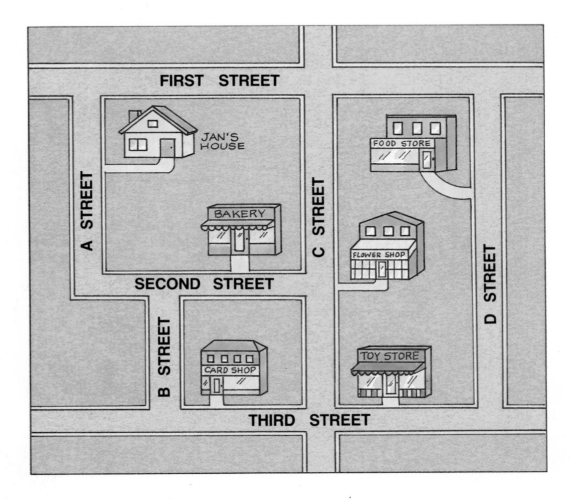

a. If you are at the food store and want to go to the bakery, which routes could you take?

b. If you want to go to the toy store from the bakery, which routes could you take?

c. If you are at the toy store and want to go to Jan's house, which routes could you take?

3. **Reviewing Calendars**
   Use the calendar to answer the questions.

a. What month does the calendar show?

b. How many days are in the month?

c. What special day is on the first Tuesday?

d. On which day of the week is January 24?

Activity

Make a list of four things that you would find at each of these neighborhood places.

City Hall

TERRYVIL[LE]
CITY HA[LL]

rule

Line up here for tour

Buy a new police car?

YES   NO
||| ||

vote

GUIDE

NO PARKING

law

leader

Working Together

People Work Together

People belong to many groups. Groups are made up of people who share something that is the same. A family is a group. A class at school is a group. The people in a neighborhood are also a group. To what groups do you belong?

People in groups work together. They help each other. They take turns and share. When people in a group work together, the group can do more things.

How are the people in this group working together to help others?

Name two things people in groups can do to work together.

The
Bundle
of
Sticks

A Fable by Aesop   Retold by Loretta Kaim

This is a story about a father who teaches his four children a lesson about working together as a group.

Once there was a father who had four children. He worried about his children because they were always fighting with each other.

"What can I do to show my children that fighting with one another is not good?" the father asked himself.

43

Finally the father had an idea. He took four big sticks and tied them together with a rope. Then he called his children to him.

"Who can break this bundle of sticks?" the father asked.

Each child took a turn and tried to break the bundle. But not one of the children could break it.

Then the father untied the rope holding the four sticks together. He gave each child a stick.

"Now see if you can break just one stick," the father said.

Each child broke one stick very easily.

"Children," said the father, "when you fight with each other, each of you is as weak as one of these sticks. But if you work together in a group, you will be as strong as the bundle of sticks."

Finding What Is Alike and Different

1. **TELL** which pictures are alike.

TELL which picture is different.

A   B   C

Helping Yourself

One way to find how things are alike and different is to:

- **LOOK** at the first picture to see what it shows.
- **CHOOSE** something in the picture.
- **LOOK** at the other pictures to see if they show the same thing you chose in the first picture.
- **TELL** the ways the pictures are alike or different.

2. Each picture shows some things that are alike and some things that are different. All three pictures are alike because they show the same children. Pictures **A** and **C** are alike because they show the children working together. Picture **B** is different from pictures **A** and **C**. Tell why.

3. TELL which pictures below are alike.
TELL which picture below is different.

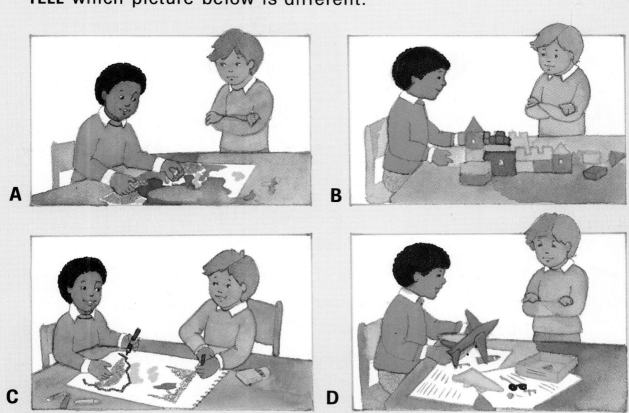

A

B

C

D

4. What steps could you use to find how things are <u>alike</u> and <u>different</u>?
How can finding how things are alike and different help you in school?

Rules and Laws

People everywhere follow **rules**. Rules tell us what to do and what not to do.

Every family has rules. Every school has rules, too. What rules are these children following?

Safety rules help to keep us from getting hurt. What safety rules do you follow?

Some rules help us to get along with others. They help us to take turns and be fair.

Rules for a community are called laws. A law is a rule that everyone must follow.

Every community has laws. Police officers make sure all people in a community follow the laws.

Some of the laws of a community are shown on signs. When people read the signs, they know what the law is.

What should you do if you see this sign? Why is this law a good law?

Some signs use symbols instead of words. Many signs have a symbol with a line through it. That means you cannot do something. What do these signs mean?

 Name two school rules.
Name two laws in your community.

Making Choices

This neighborhood park needs rules. It needs rules to help keep people safe. It needs rules to help people get along. The park needs rules to help people keep it a nice place for everyone.

52

Look carefully at the picture. What rules does this neighborhood park need? Why did you decide to choose the rules you did?

Solving Problems

People often work together to solve problems. Some problems can be solved more easily by a group.

The people in Debbie Cooper's neighborhood have a problem. There is no safe place for them to ride their bikes. The streets have many cars. Bikes are not allowed on the sidewalk or in the park.

Debbie's neighbors want to find a safe place to ride their bikes. They meet at Debbie's house to talk about the problem. The neighbors listen to each other's ideas about how to solve the problem. They decide that the park needs a bike path. A bike path will be a safe place for all the neighborhood people to ride their bikes.

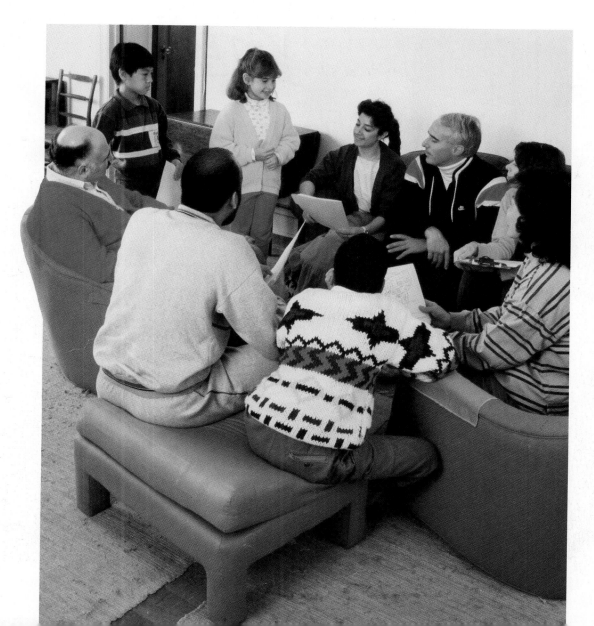

Debbie's neighbors know it will take a lot of hard work to have a bike path made in the park. The neighbors decide they need a **leader** to help them plan the work. A leader is the head of a group. A leader helps the people in a group work together.

Debbie's neighbors **vote** for a leader. To vote means to choose something. The neighbors vote for the person they think will do the best job. Which neighbor gets the most votes?

Jobs to do:
1. Ask other neighbors if they want a bike path.

2. Have neighbors who want a bike path sign their names on a list.

3. Make a map of new bike path.

4. Talk to the city's leaders.

Mrs. Mendez thanks everyone for voting for her. Then she helps everyone in the group choose a job to do. What jobs need to be done?

Debbie's neighbors know the park belongs to everyone in their city. They know they cannot make a bike path in the park themselves. The neighbors must ask the city's leaders to make the bike path.

Mrs. Mendez goes to a meeting at City Hall to talk about the bike path. City Hall is where the leaders of a city make the city's laws.

Mrs. Mendez shows the city's leaders the list of people who want a bike path in the park. She shows them the map the neighbors have made.

The city's leaders talk about the bike path and how it will help others. They decide to vote on what to do. They vote to make a bike path in the park.

These neighbors worked together to solve their problem. Now they have a safe place to ride their bikes.

Name two things the neighbors did to solve their problem.

Using a Compass Rose

Some maps have arrows to show directions.
The arrows help you to find where places are.

Other maps have a **compass rose**.
A compass rose shows directions, too.
A compass rose also helps you to find
where places are.

The **N** on the compass rose stands for north.
The **S** stands for south. The **E** stands for east.
What does the **W** stand for?

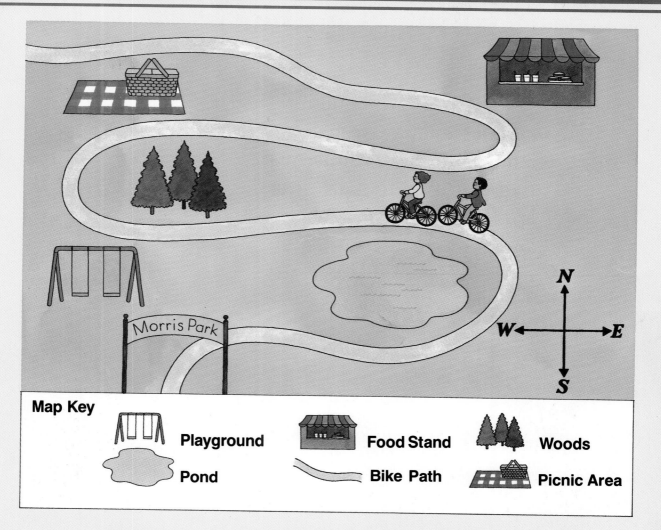

Use the compass rose on the map to answer the questions.

1. Is the park sign north or south of the Woods?
2. Is the Food Stand east or west of the Picnic Area?
3. Is the Playground east or west of the Pond?
4. Is the Picnic Area south or north of the Woods?
5. In which direction are the people riding bikes going?

Working Together in Other Lands

Paul lives in a country called Canada. He belongs to many different groups, just like you. Paul is part of a family, a class at school, and a soccer team.

Paul works together with the people in each group. His family works together to keep the house clean. His class works together to put on a show. His soccer team works together when they play a game.

The police help the people in Paul's community follow the laws. On special days the police ride horses.

Many of the people in Canada speak English. But some people in Canada speak French. Paul's family speaks French. Many signs in Canada are written in both English and French. This way, everyone in Canada can read the laws on the signs.

PLEASE KEEP OFF THE GRASS
PRIERE DE NE PAS MARCHER SUR LE GAZON

ARRÊT STOP

What groups does Paul belong to that are like groups that you belong to?
How do the groups that Paul belongs to work together?

Words You Learned

Choose one word to fill in the blanks.

City Hall	rule	leader
law	vote	

1. To _____ means to choose something.
2. A _____ is the head of a group.
3. The place where the leaders of a city make the city's laws is _____.
4. All children must walk in the halls. This is a school _____.
5. All cars must stop at a stop sign. This is a community _____.

Ideas You Learned

1. Tell about a time you worked together with someone.
2. Why are rules important?
3. How do signs help us follow the laws?
4. What would happen if the people in a group did not work together?
5. Why do groups often choose a leader?

Building Skills

1. Reviewing Alike and Different

A

B

C

D

LOOK at the pictures.

a. TELL which pictures are alike.

b. TELL which picture is different.

2. Reviewing a Compass Rose

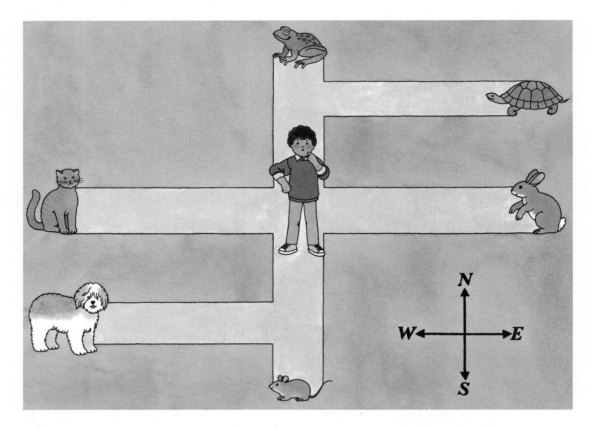

Thomas is looking for his dog, Fluffy. Use the compass rose to answer the questions.

a. Is the frog north or south of Thomas?

b. Is the cat east or west of Thomas?

c. Is the rabbit east or west of Thomas?

d. Is the mouse north or south of Thomas?

e. Will Thomas find Fluffy if he walks north and then east?

f. Will Thomas find Fluffy if he walks south and then west?

Activity

The people in these pictures are working together to get a job done. Write a story that tells about the pictures.

1

2

3

factory

wants

needs

goods

volunteers

68

services

Working for Needs and Wants

taxes

Meeting Needs and Wants

All people have **needs**. Needs are the things we must have to live. We need food to stay healthy and to grow. We need clothes to protect us from the weather.

We need shelter. A shelter is a place to live. Shelters protect us from the weather, too.

We also need love and care.

People also have **wants**. Wants are things we would like to have but can live without.

How do people get the things they need and want? Some people meet some of their needs and wants by themselves.

Most people buy the things they need and want in stores. They buy things that other people have made or grown.

 Name the needs people have.
Name two wants.

Sorting Things into Groups

1. SORT the things below into two groups.

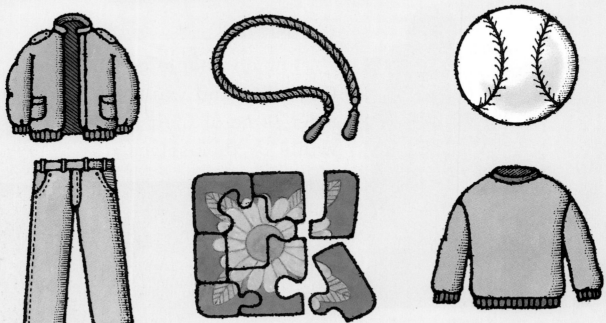

Helping Yourself

To sort means to place things together that are alike. One way to sort things into groups is to:

- **LOOK** at one thing.
- **FIND** another thing that is like it.
- **TELL** how the two things are alike.
- **NAME** the group.
- **FIND** all the things that are like these, and place them together in the group.

Repeat these steps for the other things not yet sorted.

2. You may have sorted the pants, the jacket, and the sweater into a group named "Needs." You may have sorted the puzzle, the ball, and the jump rope into a group named "Wants." What other names could you have given these groups?

3. SORT the things below into groups.

4. What steps could you use to <u>sort</u> <u>things</u> <u>into</u> <u>groups</u>? What kinds of things can you sort at school?

Earning, Spending, and Saving Money

People get, or earn, money by working at different kinds of jobs. Some people earn money by working on a farm or in a forest. Some people work at home, in a store, or in an office.

Some people earn money by working in a **factory**. A factory is a large building where things are made. Workers in factories use machines to make things like cars.

What job are these children doing to earn money?

What other jobs can people do to earn money?

After people earn money, they must choose how to use it. People may choose to spend some of their money on the things they need or want. How are these people spending the money they earned?

People may choose to save some of their money. To save money means to put money away. Some people save money until they have enough to buy something special. Some people save money to go to a special place.

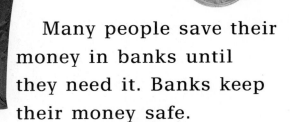

Many people save their money in banks until they need it. Banks keep their money safe.

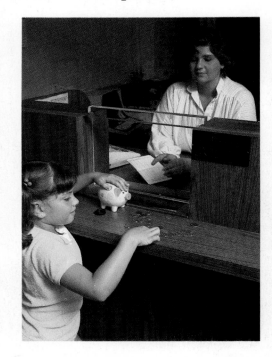

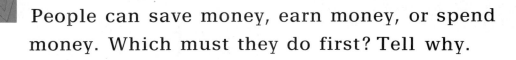

People can save money, earn money, or spend money. Which must they do first? Tell why.

77

3 Getting Goods

People use their money to buy many kinds of **goods**. Goods are things that are made or grown and then are sold. Clothes, food, toys, and books are all goods.

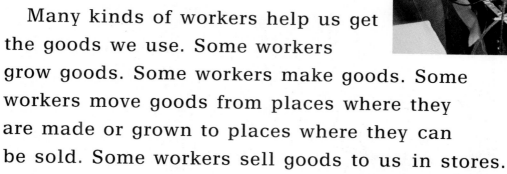

Many kinds of workers help us get the goods we use. Some workers grow goods. Some workers make goods. Some workers move goods from places where they are made or grown to places where they can be sold. Some workers sell goods to us in stores.

Name two goods that you use. Tell about one kind of worker that helps us get goods.

From Factory to You

Mr. Dennis works in this factory. He works with many other people to make American flags. Let's go inside the factory with Mr. Dennis to see how workers make the American flag.

This worker uses a machine to cut cloth to make red stripes.

80

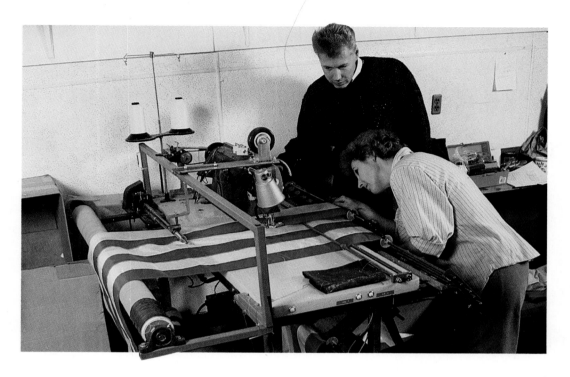

This worker sews the red and white
stripes together.

This worker sews
the stripes to blue cloth
with white stars.

This worker uses a machine to make holes on the side of the flag. The machine also puts metal rings around the holes to make them stronger.

When the flags are finished these workers fold the flags.

Finally this worker packs the flags in boxes. The boxes will be sent to places all over our country to be sold.

Maybe the American flag at your school was made by workers in this factory.

Tell about one job that a worker does to help make the American flag.

Reading Pictographs

Sandy is selling American flags at her store for a parade. She wants to know how many flags she sells each day.

Sandy uses a **pictograph** to count how many flags she sells. A pictograph is a graph that uses pictures to show numbers of things.

To read a pictograph, first read the title. The title tells what the pictograph shows. Next to the title, you will see what each picture on the pictograph stands for. When you know what each picture stands for, all you have to do is count the pictures.

American Flags Sold	🇺🇸 = 1 American Flag
Sunday	🇺🇸 🇺🇸
Monday	🇺🇸 🇺🇸 🇺🇸 🇺🇸 🇺🇸 🇺🇸
Tuesday	🇺🇸
Wednesday	🇺🇸 🇺🇸 🇺🇸 🇺🇸 🇺🇸
Thursday	🇺🇸 🇺🇸 🇺🇸
Friday	🇺🇸 🇺🇸 🇺🇸 🇺🇸 🇺🇸 🇺🇸 🇺🇸
Saturday	🇺🇸 🇺🇸 🇺🇸 🇺🇸

Count the pictures on the pictograph to answer the questions.

1. How many flags were sold on Thursday?
2. How many flags were sold on Monday?
3. On which day were the most flags sold?
4. Were more flags sold on Wednesday or Saturday?
5. Sandy's Store had 35 American flags to sell. How many flags did the store sell in all?

85

Reading Bar Graphs

There is another way that Sandy can count how many American flags she sells. She can use a **bar graph**. A bar graph is a graph that uses colored bars to show numbers of things.

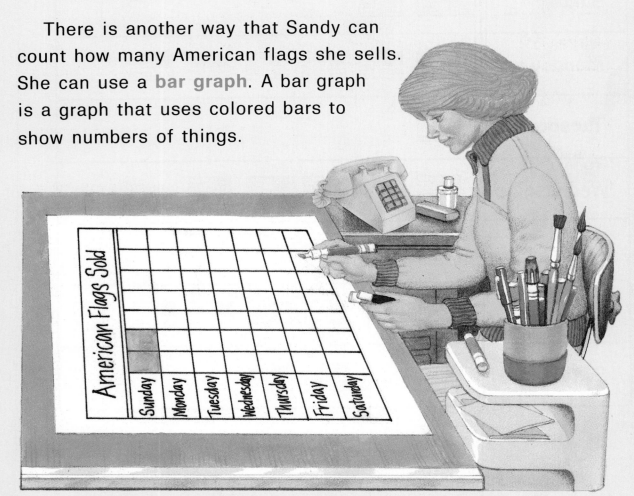

A bar graph is different from a pictograph. You do not count pictures on a bar graph. The numbers along the bottom of a bar graph tell how many things there are.

To read a bar graph, first read the title. The title tells what the bar graph shows.

American Flags Sold

Sunday							
Monday							
Tuesday							
Wednesday							
Thursday							
Friday							
Saturday							

0   1   2   3   4   5   6   7

Use the bar graph to find out how many flags were sold on Wednesday. First, find the colored bar for Wednesday. Then, move your finger along the colored bar and stop at the line where the bar ends. The number just below the line tells how many flags were sold on Wednesday.

Read the bar graph to answer the questions.
1. How many flags were sold on Saturday?
2. How many flags were sold on Sunday?
3. Were more flags sold on Tuesday or Friday?

5 Getting Services

You know that people use their money to buy goods. People also use their money to pay for services. Services are jobs that workers do for others. What jobs do these service workers do for others?

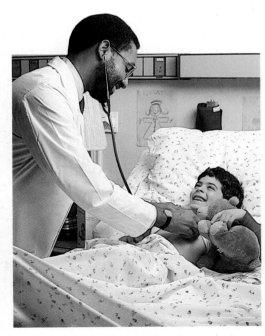

Some service workers work for a community. What jobs do these service workers do for their community?

A community pays its service workers with money from taxes. People who live in a community pay tax money to the community for services.

City Hall

Taxes

Services

91

Some service workers do not earn money for the jobs that they do. They are called **volunteers**. Volunteers work without pay because they want to help others. How are these volunteers helping others?

Name two services that you use. How is a volunteer different from other service workers?

A Special Service Worker

Mary McLeod Bethune loved to learn and to help others learn. When she was little, she and other African-American children could not go to school with other American children. There were no schools for African-American children in Mary McLeod Bethune's community until she was 11 years old. She thought it was not fair that she had to wait so long to begin school.

Mary McLeod Bethune believed that all children should be able to learn at an early age. When she grew up, she opened her own school. As a teacher in her school, Mary McLeod Bethune helped many children to learn. She worked hard so that all children would have the same chance to learn.

FLAG ON A FLAGPOLE

by Wendy Vierow

The children on Parker Street want
to buy something special for their
clubhouse. Read the play to find out
what they want and how they get the
money to buy it.

THE PLAYERS

Susie

David

Dale

Mr. and Mrs. Toplin

Sarah

Carl

Storekeeper

Place: *The Clubhouse on Parker Street*
Time: *A Saturday in October*

Susie: We really should have an American flag for our clubhouse.

Carl: I think we should buy a big flag. A very big flag!

Dale: That's a great idea! Let's buy one that's big enough to cover up one whole side of our clubhouse!

Sarah: A flag that big will cover up the windows.

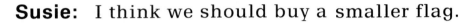

Susie: I think we should buy a smaller flag.

Sarah: I agree. We could hang a smaller flag on a flagpole by the door.

Carl: Some of us want a big flag. Some of us want a small flag. What should we do?

Susie: Let's vote on what size flag we should get.

Dale: That sounds fair.

David: Anyone who wants a big flag, raise your hand.

(Dale and Carl raise their hands.)

David: Anyone who wants a smaller flag on a flagpole, raise your hand.

(David, Susie, and Sarah raise their hands.)

Susie: More of us voted for a smaller flag on a flagpole, so that's the kind of flag we'll get.

Carl: Why did you vote for a smaller flag on a flagpole, David?

David: I like to see out of all the windows.

Carl: Oh.

Sarah: How much money does a flag on a flagpole cost?

David: I saw one in a store window for $4.50 plus tax.

Dale: How will we get $4.50 plus tax? I don't have any money.

Susie: We could earn money to buy the flag.

Carl: How can our club earn money?

Dale: We could put on a show!
I could be a queen.

David: We could sell lemonade.

30¢ a Glass

Sarah: We could do jobs for people.

Carl: What kinds of jobs?

Sarah: We could rake leaves.

Susie: That's a good idea. We
could all work together.

David: Let's see. We need $4.50 plus tax. If we charged $5.00, we would have enough money for the flag and the tax.

Carl: Let's ask our neighbors on Parker Street if they need us to rake any leaves.

(Mr. and Mrs. Toplin enter.)

Dale: Would you like our club to rake your leaves for $5.00?

Mrs. Toplin: We do have a lot of leaves.

Mr. Toplin: Let me get you some rakes.

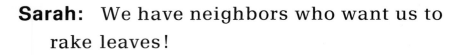

Sarah: We have neighbors who want us to rake leaves!

(Mr. Toplin leaves and comes back with five rakes.)

Susie: Let's all work together and rake the leaves into piles.

(They all work together. Mr. and Mrs. Toplin watch.)

Dale: We're done!

Mr. Toplin: Here's your $5.00.

Mrs. Toplin: You did a fine job!

David: Thank you.

(Mr. and Mrs. Toplin leave. Susie, Sarah, David, Carl, and Dale go into the store. The Storekeeper enters.)

Susie: We'd like an American flag on a flagpole, please. Like the one in the window.

Storekeeper: That flag costs $4.50 plus $.27 tax. That will be a total of $4.77.

David: Here's $5.00.

(The Storekeeper reaches to a shelf to get the flag on a flagpole.)

Storekeeper: And here's your flag on a flagpole, plus your change.

Sarah: This will look great on our clubhouse!

Dale: Let's go back right now and put it up.

BUILDING BRIDGES

Working in Other Lands

Nita and her family live in a country called India.

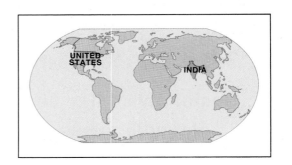

Nita has the same needs as you do. She needs food, clothing, shelter, and love and care.

Nita also has wants. She wants a kite. Nita also wants to visit the Taj Mahal. The Taj Mahal is a very large and beautiful building in India.

Nita's father works in a rug factory. Nita's mother makes clothes for others. Nita's parents work to earn money for things the family needs and wants. They use the money they earn to pay for goods and services.

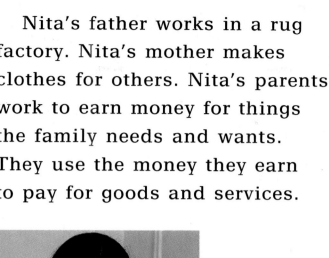

Some of the goods that are made or grown in India are sold in our country. You may see this sticker on goods from India.

What needs does Nita have that are the same as your needs?

103

Words You Learned

Choose one word to finish each sentence.

goods	**needs**	**services**	
wants	**factory**	**taxes**	**volunteers**

1. Food, clothes, shelter, and love and care are _____.
2. A kite and a trip to the zoo are _____.
3. Doctors and bus drivers provide _____.
4. Apples, shoes, puzzles, and books are _____.
5. Workers use machines to make goods in a _____.
6. People who work without pay are called _____.
7. People must pay _____ to their community for services.

Ideas You Learned

1. How are wants different from needs?
2. Why do people work?
3. Name two goods that help meet needs.
4. Name two goods people might want.
5. Tell how workers help us get goods.

Building Skills

1. Reviewing Pictographs

Tony is a service worker. He gives people haircuts at the barber shop.

Haircuts Given by Tony	✂ = 1 Haircut
Sunday	
Monday	✂ ✂
Tuesday	✂ ✂
Wednesday	✂ ✂ ✂ ✂ ✂
Thursday	✂ ✂ ✂
Friday	✂ ✂ ✂ ✂
Saturday	✂ ✂ ✂ ✂ ✂ ✂

Read the pictograph to answer the questions.

a. What does the pictograph show?

b. How many haircuts did Tony give on Wednesday?

c. How many haircuts did Tony give on Friday?

d. On which day did Tony give the most haircuts?

2. Reviewing Bar Graphs

Tassai saved these coins.

Coins Tassai Saved							
Pennies							
Nickels							
Dimes							
Quarters							
	0	1	2	3	4	5	6 7

Read the bar graph to answer the questions.

a. What does the bar graph show?

b. How many pennies did Tassai save?

c. How many nickels did Tassai save?

d. How many dimes did Tassai save?

e. Did Tassai save more nickels or more dimes?

f. How many coins did Tassai save in all?

3. Reviewing Sorting

SORT the things below into two groups.

What names can you give these groups?

Activity

Draw a picture of a worker. Write a sentence at the bottom of your picture that tells about the worker and the job that he or she does.

I am a cook at Danny's Sandwich Shop.

UNIT

4

Living on the Earth

desert

natural resources

People Live in Many Places

People live in many places. You know that Americans live in communities.

Americans also live in places called states. A state is made up of many communities. This map shows some communities in the state of Arizona.

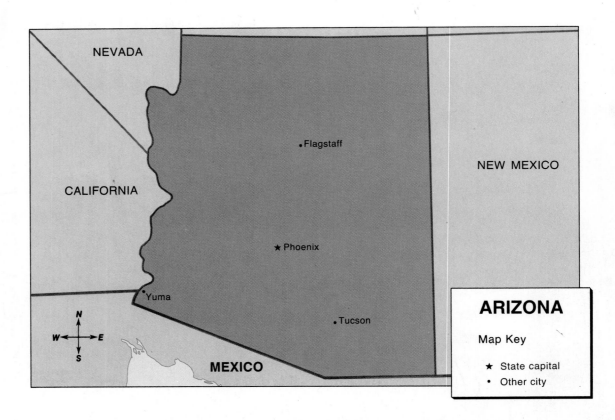

ARIZONA

Map Key

★ State capital

• Other city

Each state has one special city called a capital. The capital city is where the state leaders work. Find the capital city of Arizona on the map.

ARIZONA
◆ S T A T E S Y M B O L S ◆

State Flag

State Flower
Giant Saguaro Cactus

State Bird
Cactus Wren

State Tree
Paloverde

Each state has special symbols like a flag, flower, bird, and tree. These symbols all stand for the state of Arizona.

Americans live in communities and in states. Americans also live in a country called the United States of America. The United States is made up of 50 states.

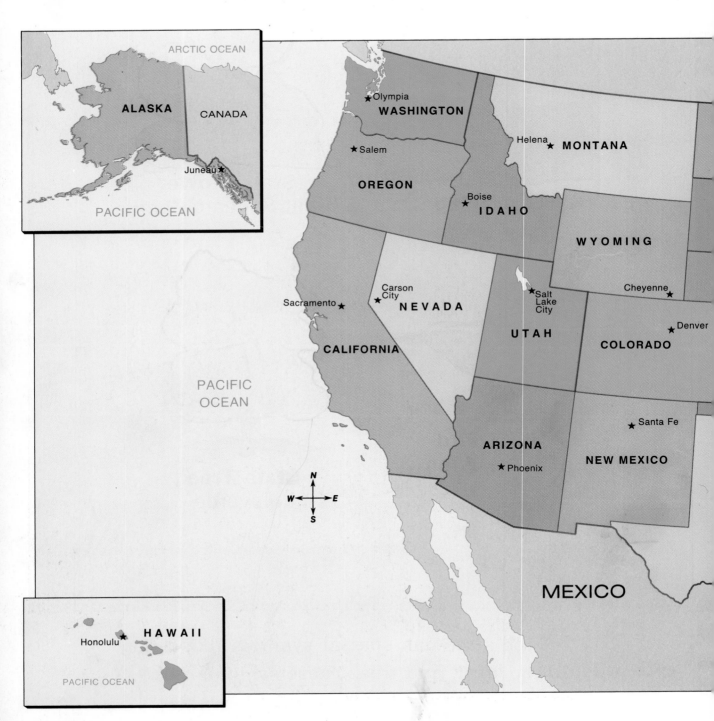

This map shows each state and its capital. Find your state on the map. What is the capital of your state?

 Name three places where Americans live.

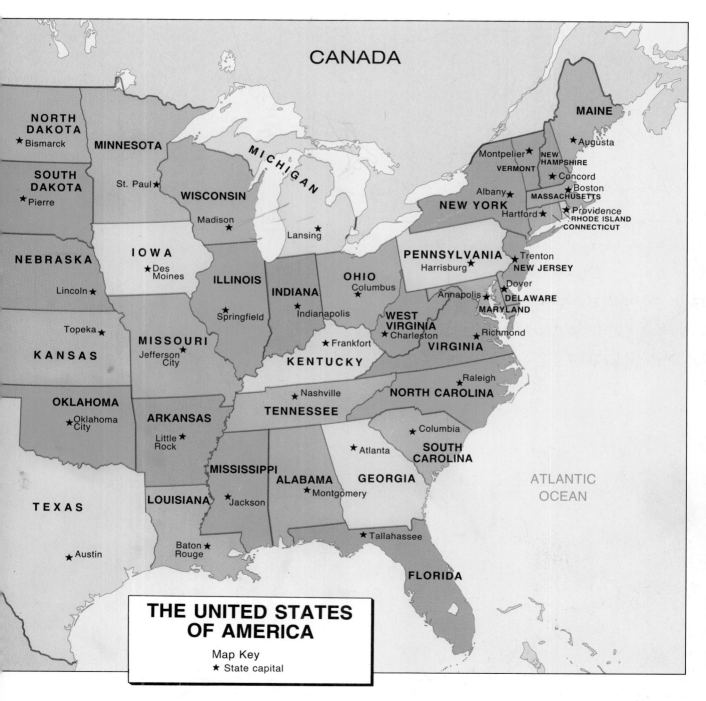

THE UNITED STATES OF AMERICA

Map Key

★ State capital

2 Our Place on the Earth

Americans live in a community, a state, and a country. Americans and all people live in another place. We all live on the earth.

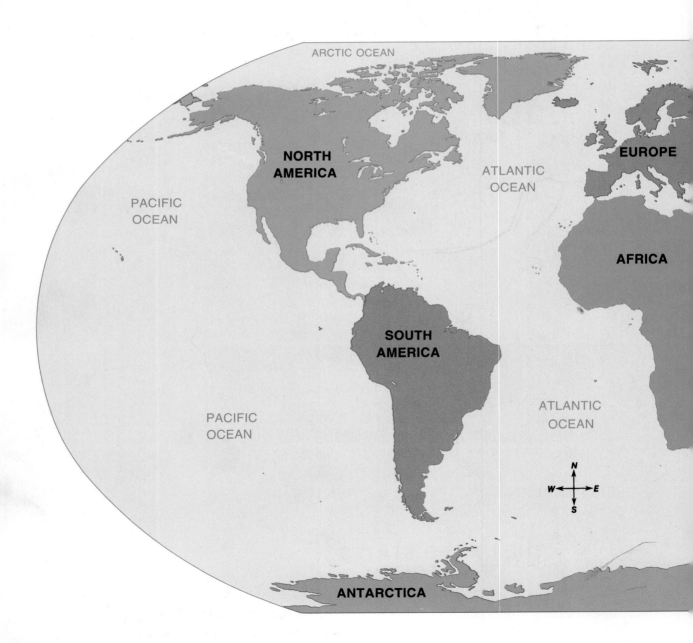

114

The earth is made up of land and water. The land on the earth is made up of seven **continents**. A continent is a very large body of land. Find and name the seven continents on the map.

The waters around the continents are **oceans**. An ocean is a very large body of salt water. There are four oceans on the earth.

Find and name the four oceans on the map.

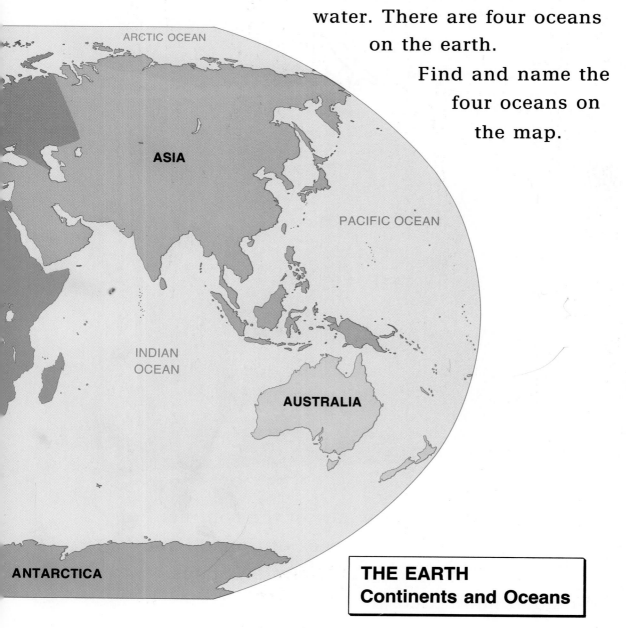

ARCTIC OCEAN

ASIA

PACIFIC OCEAN

INDIAN OCEAN

AUSTRALIA

ANTARCTICA

THE EARTH
Continents and Oceans

Greetings from *CANADA*

Greetings from *Mexico*

The United States is part of the continent of North America. The countries of Canada and Mexico are neighbors of the United States. Canada and Mexico are part of North America, too.

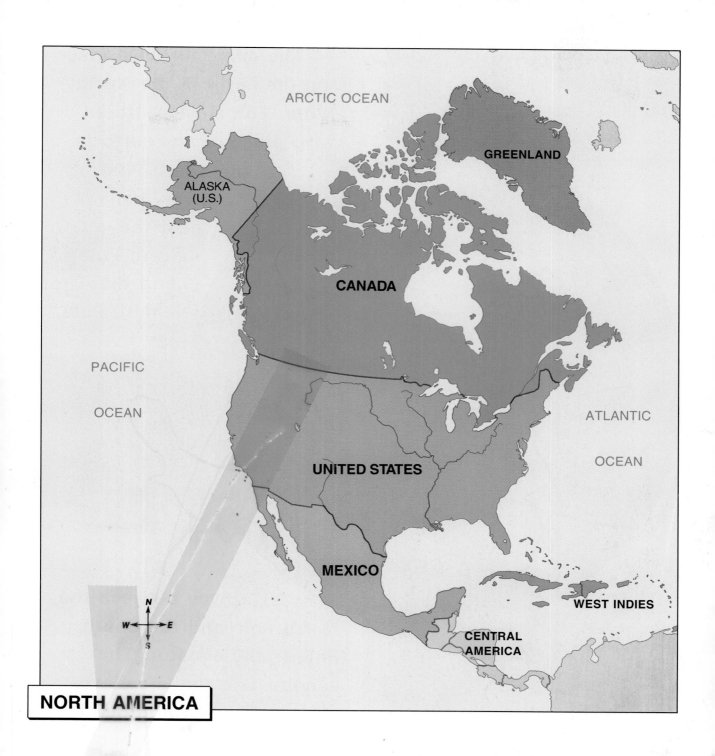

ARCTIC OCEAN

GREENLAND

ALASKA
(U.S.)

CANADA

PACIFIC

OCEAN

ATLANTIC

OCEAN

UNITED STATES

N
W — E
S

MEXICO

WEST INDIES

CENTRAL
AMERICA

NORTH AMERICA

Find the United States on the map.

Which country is our neighbor to the north?

Which country is our neighbor to the south?

North Pole

Equator

South Pole

The most northern place on the earth is the North Pole. The most southern place on the earth is the South Pole. It is very cold near the North Pole and the South Pole.

Halfway between the North Pole and the South Pole is the equator. The equator is a make-believe line around the middle of the earth. It is very hot in places near the equator.

 On which continent is the United States?

118

A Person Who Saw the Earth from Space

Sally Ride worked very hard to become an astronaut. An astronaut is a person who travels into space. Space is the area far above the earth.

Sally Ride and four other astronauts traveled into space in a spaceship called *Challenger*. She was the very first American woman to travel into space and to see the earth from space. Sally Ride worked hard to do something no other woman had done before. Her hard work has made it easier for other women to become astronauts.

Understanding Day and Night

The earth is always turning in space. As the earth turns, day changes to night. Night changes to day.

The sun can only shine on one side of the earth at a time. It is light on the side of the earth that faces the sun. It is day on that side of the earth.

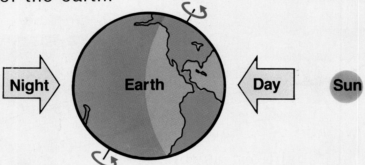

When it is light on one side of the earth, it is dark on the other side. The dark side of the earth faces away from the sun. It is night on that side of the earth.

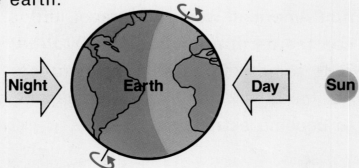

You can use a flashlight and a globe to show day and night. Look at the picture. Is it day or night on the side of the earth marked **A**?

Is it day or night on the side of the earth marked **B**?

Land and Water

All people live on the earth. But people live on different kinds of land. There are many kinds of land on the earth.

One kind of land is called a **plain**. A plain is flat land. Most plains are good for farming.

A hill is higher than
a plain. Hills rise above
the land around them.

Mountains are much higher than hills.
Mountains are the highest kind of land.

A **valley** is lower than the land around it. A valley is low land between hills or mountains.

Most **deserts** are dry, sandy places. Deserts have very little rain. Many deserts are hot in the day and cool at night.

Land that has water all around it is called an island. Islands can be large or small.

A peninsula is land that has water on three sides. One side of a peninsula is joined to a larger body of land.

There are different kinds of bodies of water on the earth, too. You know that oceans are the largest bodies of salt water.

Another kind of body of water is a **river**. A river is a long body of water that flows across the land. Most rivers flow into a larger body of water, like an ocean.

A **lake** is a body of water with land all around it. A lake is much smaller than an ocean. Lakes are made up of fresh water or salt water.

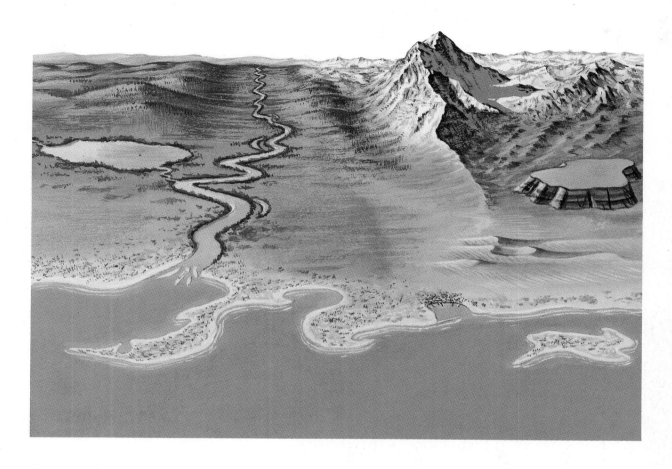

This picture shows different kinds of
land and water. Match each word below to
the part of the picture that it tells about.

plain	hill	mountain	valley	desert
island	peninsula	river	lake	ocean

 Which kind of land has water all around it?

Which kind of water has land all around it?

Reading Landform Maps

The different kinds of land are called **landforms**. A landform map can show landforms such as plains, hills, and mountains. Landform maps use color symbols to show these different kinds of land.

Most landform maps use the color green to show plains.

The color tan is often used to show hills.

Orange is often used to show mountains.

128

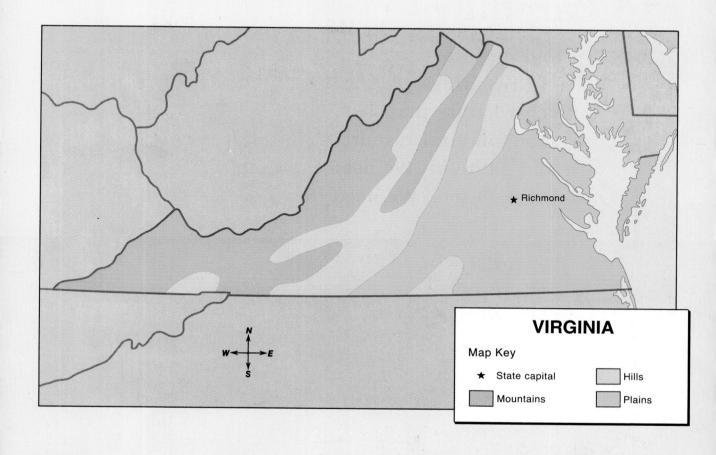

Use the landform map to answer the questions about the state of Virginia.

1. What kinds of land are shown on the map?

2. On what kind of land is the state capital?

3. In what part of the state are mountains?

4. What kind of land is between the plains and mountains in Virginia?

LESSON 4
Using Natural Resources Carefully

Land and water on the earth are important **natural resources**. Natural resources are things in nature that people use. The earth has many natural resources, like soil, water, air, and sunlight. We need these natural resources to live. We need them to grow food.

THINGS MADE FROM TREES

Trees grow on the earth's land. Trees are an important natural resource, too. After trees are cut down, what are some things that can be made from them?

It is important that people use natural resources carefully. We must be careful to plant new trees when we cut trees down. Trees take a very long time to grow.

We must be careful not to waste our natural resources. We must also be careful to keep natural resources, like air and water, clean.

 Name two natural resources.

Asking Questions

1. Mrs. White works in one of our country's parks. If she was a visitor in your class, what questions would you ask her?

Helping Yourself

When you ask questions, you want to find out something. One way to ask questions is to:

- **CHOOSE** something that you want to know more about.
- **ASK YOURSELF:** What do I want to know?
- **USE** question starters like <u>who</u>, <u>what</u>, <u>when</u>, <u>where</u>, <u>why</u>, and <u>how</u>.
- **LIST** questions that will get you the information that you want to know.

2. If you want to know about resources, you may ask Mrs. White these questions:
- <u>What</u> kind of resources are in the park?
- <u>How</u> do you take care of the resources in the park?

What other questions could you ask about resources?

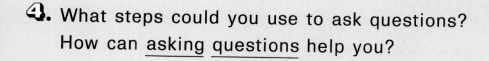

3. What questions could you ask if you want to know about these things?
- Mrs. White's job
- landforms in the park
- animals in the park

4. What steps could you use to ask questions? How can <u>asking</u> <u>questions</u> help you?

Words You Learned

Tell if each sentence is true or false.

1. A <u>capital</u> is where state leaders work.
2. A <u>plain</u> is higher than the land around it.
3. A <u>mountain</u> is the highest kind of land.
4. A <u>valley</u> is higher than a hill.
5. A <u>desert</u> has very little rain.
6. Land that has water on three sides only is an <u>island</u>.
7. A <u>lake</u>, a <u>river</u>, and a <u>peninsula</u> are all bodies of water.
8. The largest bodies of salt water are <u>oceans</u>.
9. North America is one of the seven <u>continents</u>.
10. Water, sunlight, and soil are <u>natural</u> <u>resources</u>.

Ideas You Learned

1. How many states make up the United States?
2. What are the large bodies of land that make up the earth called?
3. Tell how an island and a peninsula are different.
4. Tell how a lake and an ocean are different.
5. Tell two ways we can use our natural resources carefully.

Building Skills

1. Reviewing Day and Night

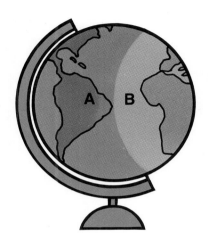

a. Is it day or night on the side of the earth marked **A**? Write a sentence that tells why.

b. Is it day or night on the side of the earth marked **B**? Write a sentence that tells why.

2. Reviewing Landform Maps

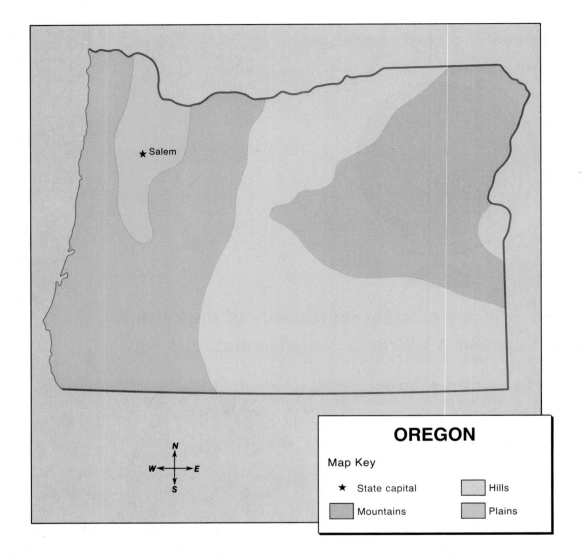

Use the landform map to answer these questions about the state of Oregon.

a. On what kind of land is the state capital?

b. Are there more plains or mountains in Oregon?

c. What kinds of land are in the east part of Oregon?

3. Reviewing Asking Questions

If an astronaut was a visitor in your class, what three questions could you ask this visitor?

LIST your questions.

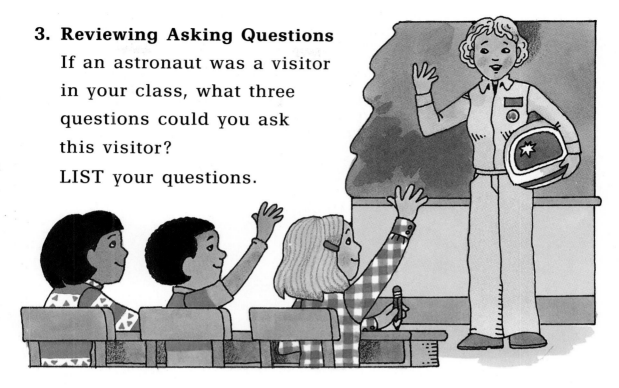

Activity

Your address shows that you live in many places. Write your address on a piece of paper. Circle all the different places where you live.

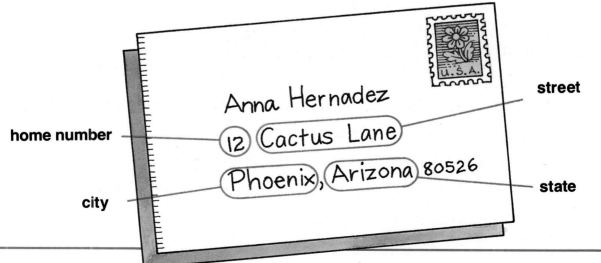

street

home number

Anna Hernadez

12 Cactus Lane

Phoenix, Arizona 80526

state

city

village

settlement

President

settlers

colonies

history

UNIT 5

pioneers

America Long Ago

museum

Learning About the Past

History is the story of the past. Our country's history tells about places and people. It tells about things that happened in America long ago.

You can learn about our country's history in many ways. You can visit places that look like they did long ago. You can read books about our country's past.

You can see things from our country's past in **museums**. A museum is a place where people can go to see interesting things.

You can also learn about our past by listening to people tell stories about what it was like to live in our country long ago.

✔ Tell two ways you can learn about our country's history.

The First Americans

The first people to live in America were the Indians. They lived in groups in different parts of America.

One big group of Indians was called the Powhatan. Find the Powhatan on the map.

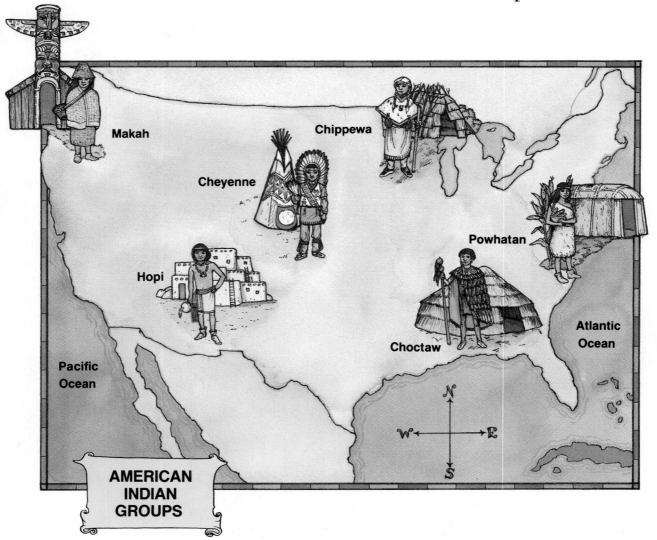

Makah

Chippewa

Cheyenne

Hopi

Powhatan

Choctaw

Pacific Ocean

Atlantic Ocean

N
W ← → E
S

AMERICAN INDIAN GROUPS

144

The Powhatan lived in **villages**. A village is a community that is smaller than a town. There were many homes in each Powhatan village. A large fence was built around the villages to help keep them safe places to live.

The Powhatan grew corn, beans, and other vegetables in fields close to their villages. They also hunted wild animals for food and used the animals' hides to make their clothes.

Pocahontas was a Powhatan princess. She helped the Powhatan and the new people who came to America to get along and to become friends.

The song on the next page is part of an Indian stick game.

INDIAN STICK SONG

Ma koo - ay Ko tay - o Ay - koo-ee tah - nah.

Ma koo - ay Ko tay - o Ay - koo-ee tah - nah.

Use sticks or pencils to play this stick game
with a partner. Follow these directions.

7 Repeat steps 1 through 6 three more times
to finish the song.

How did the Powhatan meet their need
for food?

LESSON 3
The Jamestown Settlement

The Indians were the only people who lived in America until the first settlers came. Settlers were people who came from other countries to live in America.

Some settlers sailed to America from a country called England. They landed close to where the Powhatan lived. The settlers named the place where they landed Jamestown. Jamestown is in the state we now call Virginia.

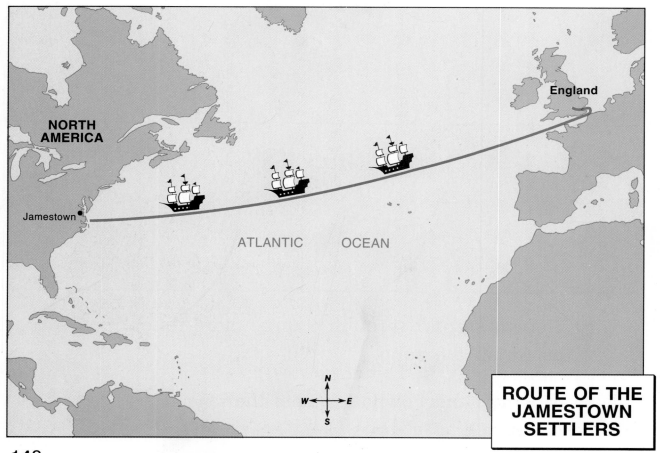

ROUTE OF THE JAMESTOWN SETTLERS

148

The settlers worked together to build a **settlement** at Jamestown. A settlement is a small community built by settlers. The Jamestown settlers had many things to do.

The settlers had to meet their need for shelter. First, they had to cut down trees to clear the land. Then, they used the trees to build homes and a fort to keep them safe.

The settlers also had to meet their needs
for food and clothing. They fished and hunted
for food. They planted corn and other
vegetables. They made their own clothes.

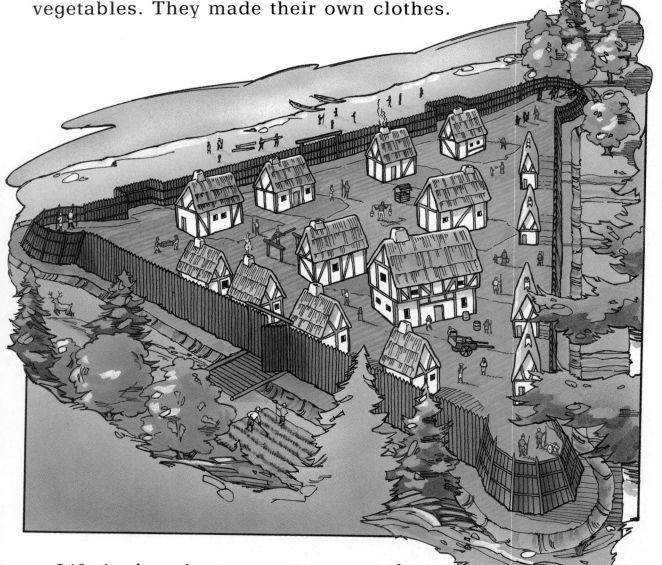

Life in America was not easy, and
many times the Jamestown settlers thought of
sailing back to England. In the end, they decided
to stay and Jamestown became the first lasting
English settlement in America.

Today Jamestown looks like it did
long ago when the early settlers lived there.
People from all over like to
visit Jamestown to see what
life was like in the past.

Why do we remember the settlement
at Jamestown?

Reading Diagrams

A **diagram** is a drawing that shows the parts of something. This drawing is a diagram that shows some parts of the *Godspeed,* one of the ships that carried the Jamestown settlers to America. Look at the diagram. Find the ship's compass. Find the back of the ship called the stern.

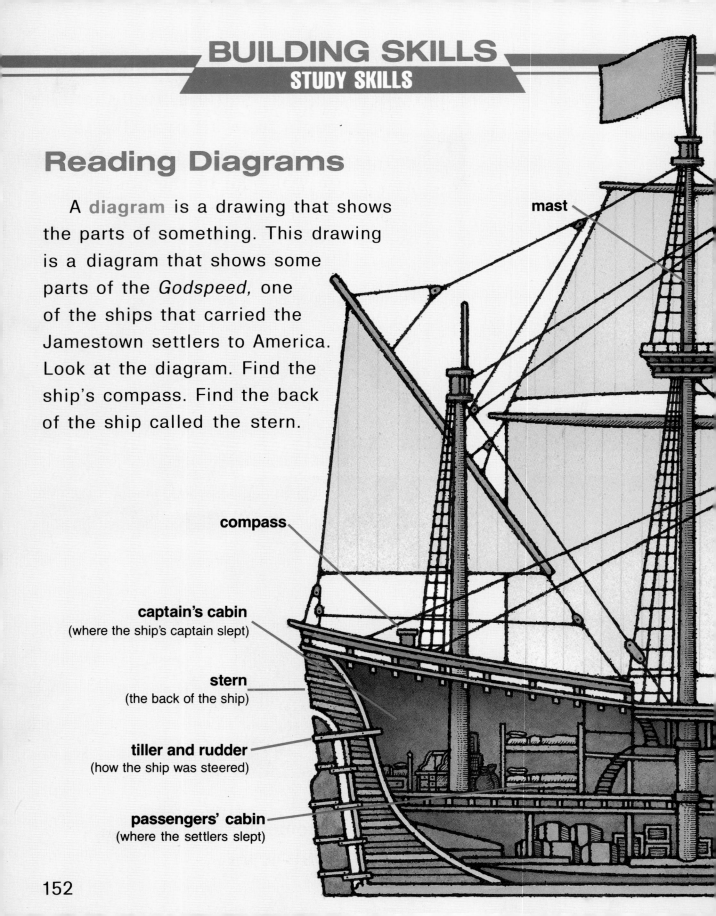

mast

compass

captain's cabin
(where the ship's captain slept)

stern
(the back of the ship)

tiller and rudder
(how the ship was steered)

passengers' cabin
(where the settlers slept)

Use the diagram to answer the questions.

1. How many masts did the ship have?
2. Where did the settlers sleep?
3. What is the front of the ship called?
4. Where was food and water kept?
5. Was the captain's cabin in the bow or stern?

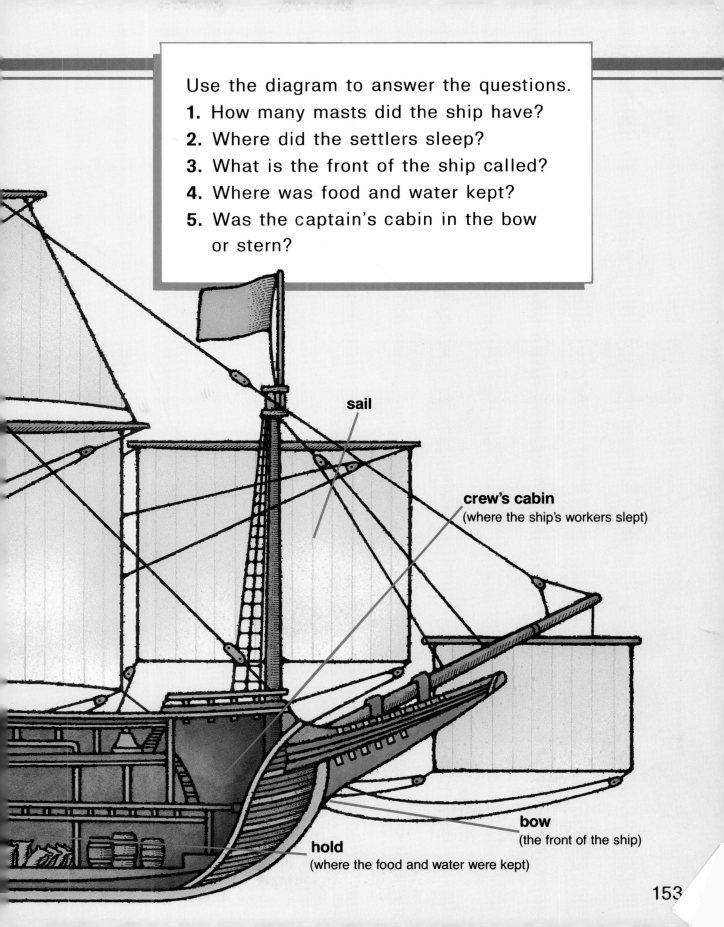

sail

crew's cabin
(where the ship's workers slept)

bow
(the front of the ship)

hold
(where the food and water were kept)

153

Fighting to Be Free

The settlers at Jamestown were not the only English settlers who came to America to live. Later, other English settlers called Pilgrims came to America. They built a settlement called Plymouth in the state we now call Massachusetts.

After a hard year, the Pilgrims had a feast and gave thanks to God and to the Indians who helped them. We remember this feast every year when we celebrate Thanksgiving.

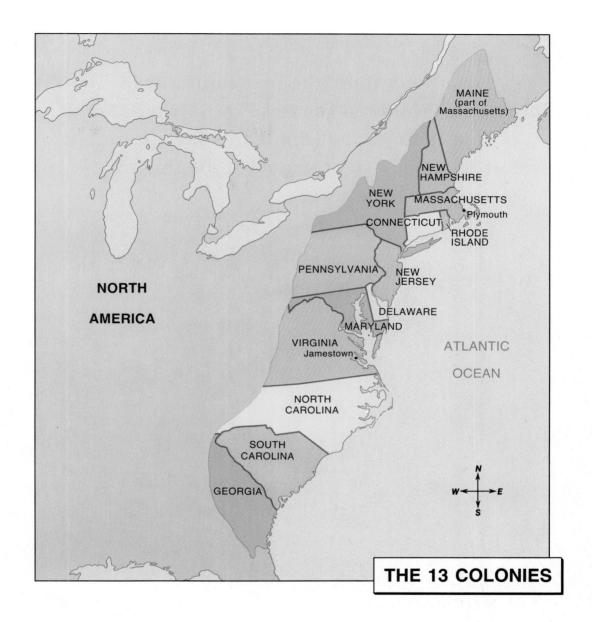

THE 13 COLONIES

As time went by, more and more settlers came to America. Soon there were settlements all along the Atlantic Ocean.

The settlements were parts of 13 colonies. A colony is a place that must follow the laws of another country. The people who lived in the 13 colonies had to follow the laws made by England.

For a long time, the people in the 13 colonies followed the laws of England. Many people thought that England's laws were not fair for them. They wanted to be free to make their own laws.

On July 4, 1776, they told the king of England that they were going to be a new, free country. They called their new country the United States of America.

The king of England did not want the colonies to be free. He sent soldiers to America to fight against the Americans who wanted to be free. America and England had a war. George Washington led the Americans in the fight against the English. The war lasted for many years. Finally, the Americans won the war. They were free from England.

The Granger Collection

George Washington

Now that the United States was a free country, it needed a leader. Since George Washington led Americans in the fight to be free, they wanted him to be their leader. They voted for him to be the first **President** of the United States. The President is the most important leader in our country.

Why did the king of England send soldiers to America?

What happened after the Americans won the war against England?

A Person Who Helped Our Country to Be Free

The Granger Collection

Paul Revere lived when Americans had to follow the laws of England. He wanted to live in a free country that had its own laws. Paul Revere decided to take part in America's war against England.

One night, Paul Revere made a very important ride on his horse. He rode through many settlements warning Americans that soldiers from England were coming to fight with them. He shouted, "The British are coming! The British are coming!"

The Granger Collection

Because of Paul Revere, Americans were not surprised when the English soldiers came. They were ready to fight against the English to be free.

159

LESSON 5

Pioneer Life

Over many years, more people came to live in the United States. Most people settled in the East near the Atlantic Ocean.

As the East became crowded, pioneers began to move west. A pioneer is a person who leads the way into a new land. The pioneers traveled west on trails looking for land where they could live.

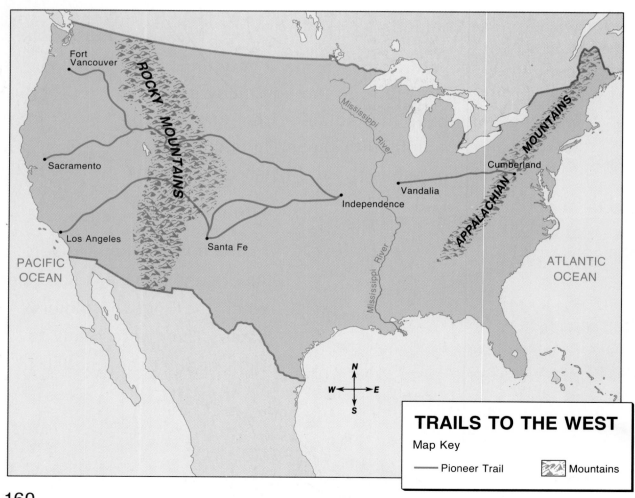

Fort Vancouver

ROCKY MOUNTAINS

Mississippi River

APPALACHIAN MOUNTAINS

Sacramento

Cumberland

Vandalia

Independence

Los Angeles

Santa Fe

Mississippi River

PACIFIC OCEAN

ATLANTIC OCEAN

N
W E
S

TRAILS TO THE WEST

Map Key

— Pioneer Trail   Mountains

This is a story about a young pioneer who traveled west with his family.

My name is John. When I was seven years old, my father and mother decided to move from Missouri to Oregon. In Oregon there was free land for farming.

Before we left, we made a big wagon and put all of our things in it. We could only bring things we needed, like food, clothes, blankets, tools, pots, and pans.

We traveled west on the Oregon Trail with 50 other families. It was safer to travel in a group. Life on the trail was hard, but the people in the group helped each other.

Every morning the men got the oxen ready to pull the wagons. The women built fires and made breakfast. We traveled all day. At night, the wagons made a circle. We were safe from danger inside the circle. After dinner, we all sang songs and told stories.

It took us six months to get to Oregon. My parents built the farm that they always wanted. Soon after we settled in Oregon, the railroad was built. Then settlers could travel west by train in just a few days.

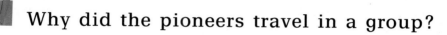 Why did the pioneers travel in a group?

Putting Things in Order

1. **PUT** the pictures in order to tell a story.

Helping Yourself

One way to put things in order is to:

- **LOOK** at each thing.
- **DECIDE** in what kind of order you want to put the things, like size, shape, or by time.
- **FIND** the thing that comes first.
- **FIND** the thing that comes next.
- **FIND** the thing that comes last.

2. You may have put the pictures in this order:
- First, the pioneers built a wagon.
- Next, the pioneers packed their needs and wants in the wagon.
- Last, the pioneers began their trip west.

3. PUT these pictures in order to show what the pioneers did from breakfast to night.

4. What steps could you use to put things in order? What things can you put in order at school?

Words You Learned

Read the words in the box. Use the words to answer the questions.

history	villages	colonies	settlers
President	settlement	pioneers	museum

1. Who is the most important leader of our country?
2. What small communities did the Powhatan Indians live in?
3. Who came from other countries to America to live?
4. What was Jamestown?
5. What places must follow the laws of another country?
6. Who leads the way into a new land?
7. Where can you go to see interesting things?
8. What is the story of the past called?

Ideas You Learned

1. Who were the first people to live in America?
2. Where was the first lasting English settlement in our country?
3. Which country's laws did the 13 colonies have to follow?
4. What things did the pioneers take with them?

Building Skills

1. Reviewing Diagrams

Many American Indians who lived in the East lived in longhouses. Longhouses were shared by more than one family. This diagram shows the area where one family lived in a longhouse.

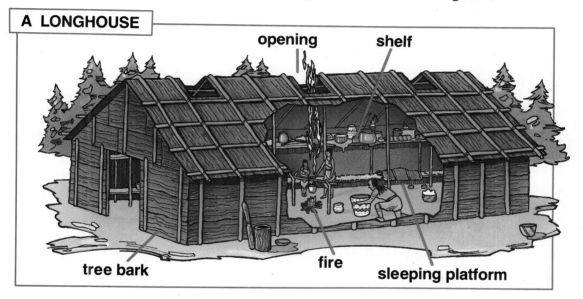

A LONGHOUSE

opening   shelf

tree bark   fire   sleeping platform

Use the diagram to answer the questions.

a. Where could the family store pots, clothes, and tools?

b. Where did the family cook?

c. What was the outside of the longhouse made from?

d. How did smoke from the fire leave the longhouse?

e. Where did the family sleep?

2. Reviewing Putting Things in Order

PUT the pictures in order to tell a story.

Activity

Paul Revere rode his horse through many settlements warning people that English soldiers were coming to fight. Pretend that you were alive when Paul Revere made his famous midnight ride. Write a story that tells what you saw and heard when Paul Revere rode past your house. Draw a picture to go with your story.

Paul Revere's Ride

I saw a man on a horse. He was riding very fast. I heard the horse's feet go "Clip clop, Clip clop."

A Dark Night

I was sleeping. I heard someone shouting, "The British are coming! The British are coming!" I ran to the window. I saw a man go by on a horse.

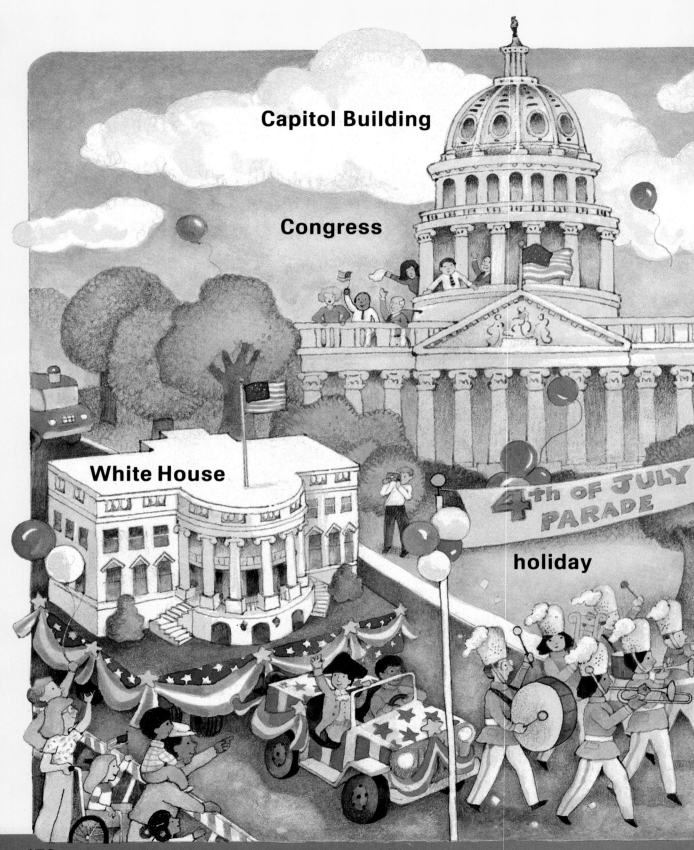

Capitol Building

Congress

White House

4th OF JULY PARADE

holiday

170

UNIT
6

Celebrating America

monument

1776

Washington, D.C.

My name is Carol. I live in an important American city called Washington, D.C. It is the capital of the United States. It is where our country's leaders work.

There are many places to visit in Washington, D.C. One special place is the White House. The White House is where the President lives and works. The President is the most important leader of our country. Americans vote to choose our President.

Another place to visit is the **Capitol Building**. The Capitol Building is where the members of **Congress** work. Members of Congress make our country's laws. The people of each state vote for leaders to be members of Congress.

There are many museums in Washington, D.C., where you can learn about history and see many interesting things. My favorite is the Air and Space Museum. It has many airplanes and spaceships.

At the National Museum of Natural History you can learn about people, places, and things from the past.

I like to visit many of the monuments in Washington, D.C. A monument is built to honor a person or something that happened.

This monument is called the Washington Monument. It honors George Washington, who was the first President of our country. From inside the top of the Washington Monument, you can see many of the special places in this city.

My favorite monument is the Lincoln Memorial. It honors Abraham Lincoln who was our country's 16th President. Abraham Lincoln lived when many African–Americans in our country were not free. When Abraham Lincoln became President, he helped to make them free.

 Name three places in Washington, D.C. Tell why they are special.

2 Places from Our Past

Washington, D.C., is only one place where people can learn about our country's history. People can also visit many other places in the United States to learn about our past.

Our country's most famous statue stands on an island that is part of New York City, New York. The Statue of Liberty is a symbol of being free. It stands for all the people who came to our country to be free.

The Gateway Arch is in St. Louis, Missouri. St. Louis is known as the "Gateway to the West" because many pioneers who traveled west began their trip in St. Louis.

The Alamo is in San Antonio, Texas. The Alamo was a fort where the people of Texas once fought to be free from the country of Mexico. After Texas became free, it became part of the United States.

 Tell about the history of one of the places in this lesson.

People from Our Past

There are many famous places in our country. There are also many famous people from our past.

Long ago Christopher Columbus sailed across the Atlantic Ocean to America from the country of Spain.

Because of Columbus, other people soon came to live in America.

Later, Benjamin Franklin was one of the many people who helped our country become free from England. He also started the first library and the first volunteer fire department in America.

180

The Granger Collection

Harriet Tubman lived when many states had laws that said African–Americans were not free. Harriet Tubman helped many African–Americans find their way to other states where they could be free.

Susan B. Anthony lived when the law said that women could not vote. She thought that this was not fair. Susan B. Anthony worked hard to change the law so that women could vote.

These people all worked hard to help America to grow. You can help America to grow, too. You can make a difference.

 Tell why one of the people in this lesson is famous.

Predicting

1. When Benjamin Franklin lived, most homes had fireplaces that were used for heat. Most of the time, the fires made too much smoke and did not make enough heat to keep people warm.

Benjamin Franklin always had new ideas. He thought to himself, "I'll do something about this problem."

What do you think happened next?

Helping Yourself

When you tell what you think will happen next, you **predict**. One way to predict is to:

- **THINK** about what you already know.
- **TELL** your ideas about what <u>could</u> happen next.
- **CHOOSE** what you think is likely to happen next.

2. You know that Benjamin Franklin always had new ideas. You also know that fireplaces did not heat very well. You may have predicted that Benjamin Franklin made a better fireplace for heating.

What really happened was that he made a heater called the Franklin stove. The Franklin stove could stand in the middle of any room and heat the air without smoke.

3. News of the Franklin stove spread quickly. **PREDICT** what happened next.

4. What steps could you use to <u>predict</u>? What kinds of things can you predict?

183

America's Holidays

Our country has many **holidays**. A holiday is a special day. Some holidays help us remember important people who helped America to grow. Other holidays help us remember important things that happened in America's past.

We celebrate Memorial Day at the end of May. On Memorial Day we honor people who gave their lives for our country. We remember that they died so that others could be free.

184

JULY						
S	M	T	W	T	F	S
	1	2	3	(4)	5	6
7	8	9	10	11	12	13
14	15	16	17	18	19	20
21	22	23	24	25	26	27
28	29	30	31			

Independence Day, or the Fourth of
July, is another holiday. On this holiday
we remember that on July 4, 1776,
American leaders decided that our country
should be free. On that day our country
became the United States of America.
That is why Independence Day is often called
our country's birthday.

We celebrate Labor Day on the first Monday in September. Labor is another word for work. On Labor Day we honor all the people who work in our country.

SEPTEMBER						
S	M	T	W	T	F	S
1	(2)	3	4	5	6	7
8	9	10	11	12	13	14
15	16	17	18	19	20	21
22	23	24	25	26	27	28
29	30					

On this holiday, some places have Labor Day Parades. Many people have picnics.

186

In November Americans celebrate
Thanksgiving Day. Americans give thanks
for many things on Thanksgiving.

NOVEMBER						
S	M	T	W	T	F	S
					1	2
3	4	5	6	7	8	9
10	11	12	13	14	15	16
17	18	19	20	21	22	23
24	25	26	27	(28)	29	30

On this holiday we remember the feast
that was shared by the Pilgrims and the
Indians at Plymouth long ago. At this feast
the Pilgrims thanked the Indians for
showing them how to live in this new land.
The Pilgrims thanked God for food, friends,
and their new home, America.

Most holidays are celebrated by all Americans. Some holidays are celebrated only by some Americans.

Saint Patrick's Day

Christmas

Chinese New Year

Chanukah

Name one of our country's holidays and tell why it is a special day.

189

Using Time Lines

A **time line** shows the order in which things happen. The time line below shows the seven days of the week. It also shows some things that Jenny did during Thanksgiving week. To read the time line look at the day and what happened on that day.

Sunday	Monday	Tuesday	Wednesday	Thursday	Friday	Saturday
Read a Book about Thanksgiving	Drew Pictures of Turkeys	Grandma Came	Baked Corn Bread	Thanksgiving Day	My 8th Birthday	Grandma Left

Use the time line to answer the questions.
1. What did Jenny do on Sunday?
2. What did Jenny do on Monday?
3. On what day did Jenny bake?
4. On what day was Thanksgiving?
5. How old was Jenny on Friday?

190

A time line can show the order of months, too. The time lines below show the order of some holidays in a year.

January	February	March	April	May	June
Martin Luther King, Jr.'s Birthday	Presidents' Day			Memorial Day	Flag Day

Use the first time line to answer these questions.

1. In what month is Memorial Day?

2. What holiday is in January?

3. What holiday is in February?

July	August	September	October	November	December
Independence Day		Labor Day	Columbus Day	Thanksgiving Day	

Use the second time line to answer these questions.

1. In what month is Thanksgiving Day?

2. What holiday is in July?

3. What holiday is in October?

The American flag is a symbol of our country. One way to honor, or show we are proud of, our country and our flag is to say the *Pledge of Allegiance*.

Pledge of Allegiance

I pledge allegiance to the flag
of the United States of America,
and to the Republic for which it stands,
one Nation under God, indivisible,
with liberty and justice for all.

When we say the *Pledge of Allegiance*,
we put our right hand over our heart to show
that we honor the flag and the country for
which it stands. Many schools start the day
by saying the *Pledge of Allegiance*.

Another way to honor the American flag is
to sing songs about it. This song honors our flag.

YOU'RE A GRAND OLD FLAG

Words and Music by George M. Cohan

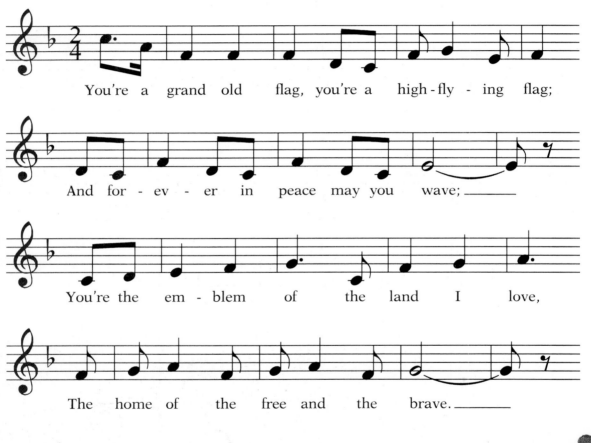

You're a grand old flag, you're a high-fly-ing flag;

And for-ev-er in peace may you wave;_____

You're the em-blem of the land I love,

The home of the free and the brave._____

Ev - ery heart beats true un - der red, white, and blue,

Where there's nev - er a boast or brag; _____

But should auld ac - quaint - ance be for - got,

Keep your eye on the grand old flag. _____

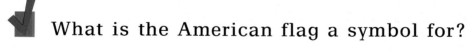

What is the American flag a symbol for?

Words You Learned

White House	Capitol Building
Congress	monuments	holidays

Choose the word that best tells about each sentence.

1. The leaders who make our country's laws belong to this group.
2. These are special days.
3. These are built to honor a person or something that happened.
4. This is where the President lives.
5. This is where our country's leaders work.

Ideas You Learned

1. What is the capital of the United States?
2. What famous statue helps us remember that many people came to America to be free?
3. What things did Benjamin Franklin do to help our country to grow?
4. Why is Independence Day often called our country's birthday?
5. Name two ways that we can honor the American flag.

Building Skills

1. Reviewing Predicting

Benjamin Franklin wanted our country
to be free. On July 4, 1776, he went to an
important meeting. At the meeting,
our country's leaders planned to sign
an important paper that said our
country was free from England.
Benjamin Franklin looked at the paper.
He held a pen in his hand.

PREDICT what happened next.

2. Reviewing Time Lines

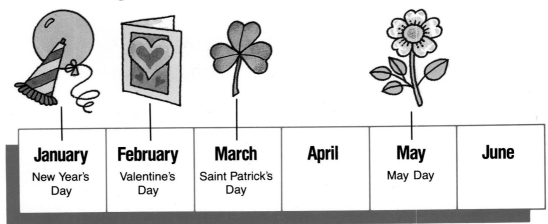

January	February	March	April	May	June
New Year's Day	Valentine's Day	Saint Patrick's Day		May Day	

Use the first time line to answer these questions.

a. What holiday is in March?

b. In what month is Valentine's Day?

c. What holiday is in January?

July	August	September	October	November	December
Independence Day		Labor Day	Columbus Day	Thanksgiving Day	

Use the second time line to answer these questions.

a. In what month is Independence Day?

b. What holiday is in September?

c. What holiday is in November?

Activity

Write a poem about your favorite American holiday. Draw a picture to go with your poem.

The 4th of July

There's a very big sound
but it's not on the ground.
I look up at the sky,
and I say "My, oh my."

Me

My brother

ATLAS

THE WORLD
Continents and Oceans

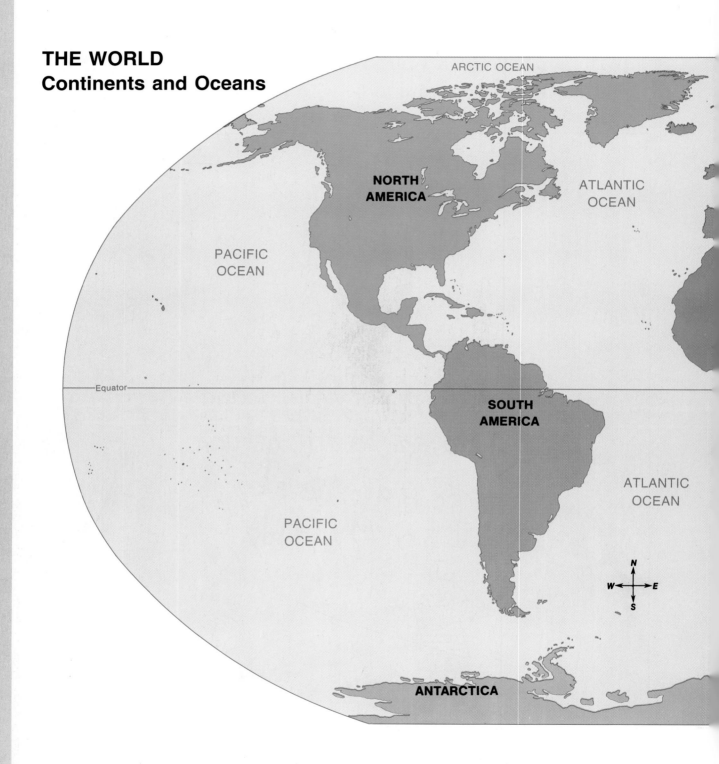

ARCTIC OCEAN

NORTH
AMERICA

ATLANTIC
OCEAN

PACIFIC
OCEAN

Equator

SOUTH
AMERICA

ATLANTIC
OCEAN

PACIFIC
OCEAN

N
W   E
S

ANTARCTICA

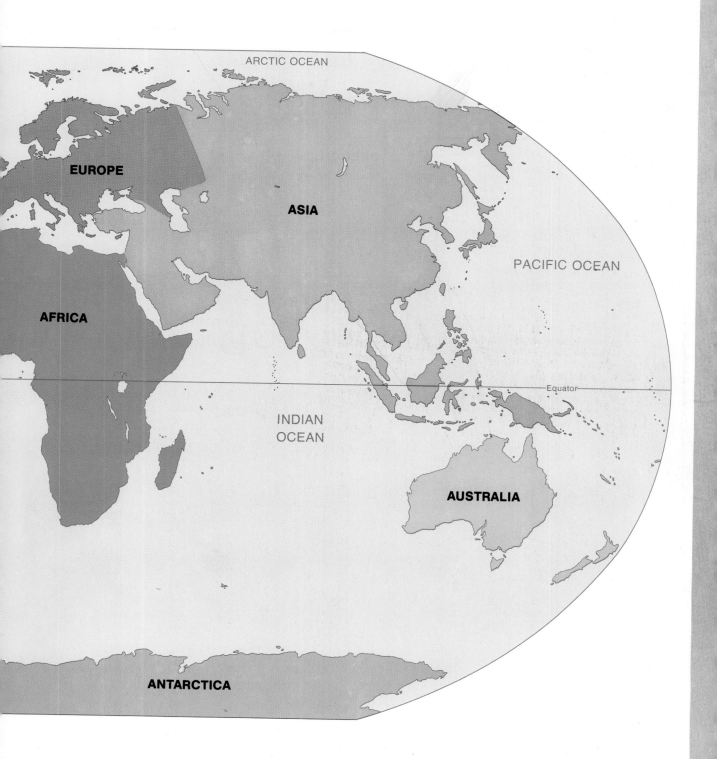

ARCTIC OCEAN

EUROPE

ASIA

PACIFIC OCEAN

AFRICA

Equator

INDIAN
OCEAN

AUSTRALIA

ANTARCTICA

ARCTIC OCEAN

ALASKA

Juneau

PACIFIC OCEAN

WASHINGTON
Olympia

Salem

OREGON

IDAHO

Boise

Helena

MONTANA

WYOMING

Cheyenne

Carson
City

Sacramento

NEVADA

Salt
Lake
City

UTAH

Denver

COLORADO

CALIFORNIA

PACIFIC
OCEAN

ARIZONA

Phoenix

Santa Fe

NEW MEXICO

MEXICO

HAWAII

Honolulu

PACIFIC OCEAN

CANADA

NORTH DAKOTA
★ Bismarck

MINNESOTA

SOUTH DAKOTA
★ Pierre

St. Paul ★

WISCONSIN

Madison ★

MICHIGAN

Lake Superior

Lake Huron

Lake Michigan

Lansing ★

MAINE
★ Augusta

Montpelier ★
VERMONT

NEW HAMPSHIRE
★ Concord
Boston

Albany ★
NEW YORK
MASSACHUSETTS

Hartford ★
Providence
RHODE ISLAND
CONNECTICUT

Lake Ontario

Lake Erie

PENNSYLVANIA
Harrisburg ★

Trenton ★
NEW JERSEY

NEBRASKA
Lincoln ★

IOWA
★ Des Moines

ILLINOIS
★ Springfield

INDIANA
Indianapolis ★

OHIO
Columbus ★

Dover
DELAWARE
Washington, D.C. ✪ ★ Annapolis
MARYLAND

KANSAS
Topeka ★

Jefferson City ★
MISSOURI

KENTUCKY
★ Frankfort

WEST VIRGINIA
★ Charleston

Richmond ★

VIRGINIA

OKLAHOMA
Oklahoma City ★

ARKANSAS
Little Rock ★

Nashville ★
TENNESSEE

NORTH CAROLINA
Raleigh ★

SOUTH CAROLINA
★ Columbia

TEXAS
★ Austin

MISSISSIPPI
Jackson ★

LOUISIANA
Baton Rouge ★

Montgomery ★
ALABAMA

★ Atlanta
GEORGIA

Tallahassee ★

ATLANTIC OCEAN

N
W ← → E
S

Gulf of Mexico

FLORIDA

THE UNITED STATES

✪ National capital   ★ State capital

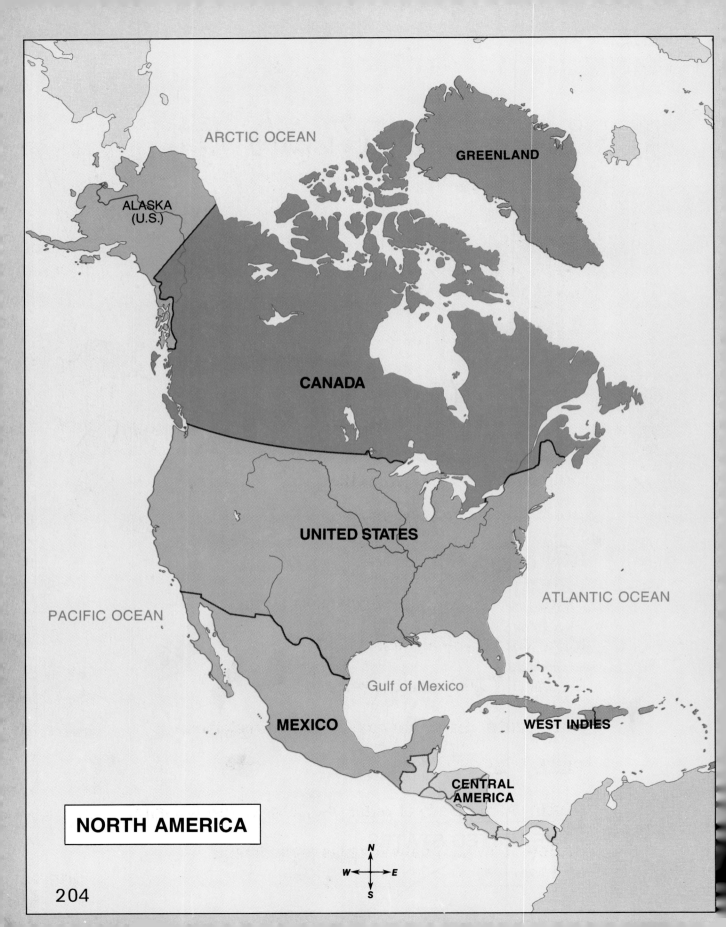

ARCTIC OCEAN

GREENLAND

ALASKA
(U.S.)

CANADA

UNITED STATES

PACIFIC OCEAN

ATLANTIC OCEAN

Gulf of Mexico

MEXICO

WEST INDIES

CENTRAL
AMERICA

NORTH AMERICA

N
W← →E
S

DICTIONARY OF
GEOGRAPHIC WORDS

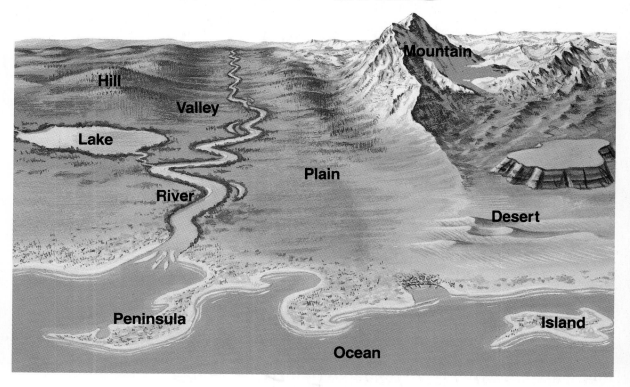

Desert A dry place with little rain.

Hill Land that rises above the land around it.

Island Land that has water all around it.

Lake A body of water with land all around it.

Mountain The highest kind of land.

Ocean A very large body of salt water.

Peninsula Land that has water on three sides.

Plain Flat land.

River A long body of water that flows across the land.

Valley Low land between hills or mountains.

PICTURE GLOSSARY

bar graph   A graph that uses colored bars to show numbers of things. This **bar graph** shows how many ducks were at Ed's Pond at different times of the day. (page 86)

calendar   A chart that shows the days, months, and weeks of the year. I circled my birthday on the **calendar**. (page 20)

capital   A city where the leaders of a state or country work. The **capital** of West Virginia is Charleston. (page 110)

Capitol Building   The building in Washington, D.C., where members of Congress work. Members of Congress make our country's laws in the **Capitol Building**. (page 174)

city   A very large community. There are many tall buildings in this **city**. (page 22)

City Hall   The building where the leaders of a city make the city's laws. The city's leaders work at **City Hall**. (page 58)

colony   A place that must follow the laws of another country. The people who lived in the 13 **colonies** had to follow the laws of England. (page 155)

community A place that has many neighborhoods. My **community** has an outdoor market where I can buy apples. (page 22)

compass rose A compass rose shows directions on a map. This **compass rose** tells me that the house is east of the lake. (page 60)

Congress Leaders who make our country's laws. **Congress** works in the Capitol Building in Washington, D.C. (page 174)

continent A very large body of land. The earth has seven **continents**. (page 115)

country A land and the people who live there. The United States of America is our **country**. (page 4)

desert A dry place with little rain. This **desert** is very sandy. (page 124)

diagram A drawing that shows parts of something. This **diagram** shows parts of a horse. (page 152)

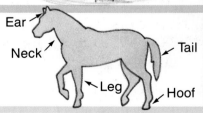

Ear
Neck
Tail
Leg
Hoof

direction North, east, south, and west are directions. Arrows can show **directions**. (page 7)

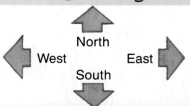

North
West
East
South

PICTURE GLOSSARY

factory   A large building where things are made. Cars are made in **factories**. (page 74)

globe A model of the earth. A **globe** looks like the earth. (page 6)

goods   Things that are made or grown and then sold. Clothes, food, and books are **goods**. (page 78)

history   The story of the past. I like to read books about our country's **history**. (page 142)

holiday   A special day. My favorite **holiday** is the Fourth of July. (page 184)

island   Land that has water all around it. We use a boat to get to the **island**. (page 125)

lake   A body of water with land all around it. We like to go fishing at the **lake**. (page 126)

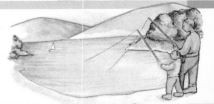

landforms   Different kinds of land. Hills, valleys, and mountains are **landforms**. (page 128)

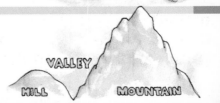

208

law A rule that everyone must follow. Some **laws** are shown on signs. (page 50)

leader The head of a group. Our group has a **leader**. (page 56)

map A drawing of a place. **Maps** show where places are. (page 2)

map key A map key tells what the symbols on a map stand for. This **map key** tells me that a red square stands for a house. (page 3)

Map Key
■ House
▬ Road
❀ Tree

monument A building or statue built to honor a person or something that happened. This **monument** honors George Washington. (page 176)

mountain The highest kind of land. There is often snow on the **mountain**. (page 123)

museum A building where people go to look at interesting things. I like to look at paintings in the **museum**. (page 143)

natural resource Something in nature that people use. Water is an important **natural resource**. (page 130)

needs Things we must have to live. Shelter, clothes, food, and love and care are **needs**. (page 70)

neighbor People who live near one another in a neighborhood. My **neighbor** lives in the house next to mine. (page 10)

neighborhood A place where people live, work, and play. This **neighborhood** has many homes. (page 10)

ocean A very large body of salt water on the earth. The earth has four **oceans**. (page 115)

peninsula Land that has water on three sides. My house is on a **peninsula**. (page 125)

pictograph A graph that uses pictures to show numbers of things. This **pictograph** shows how many times Jan rode the bus in three months. (page 84)

Jan's Bus Rides	= 1 Ride
June	🚐 🚐
July	🚐 🚐 🚐 🚐
August	🚐 🚐 🚐

pioneer A person who leads the way into a new land. The **pioneers** traveled west in covered wagons. (page 160)

plain Flat land. Our farm is on a **plain**.
(page 122)

predict To tell what might happen next. I **predict** that it will be light soon. (page 183)

President The most important leader in our country. George Washington was our country's first **President**. (page 158)

river A long body of water that flows across the land. We like to sit by the **river**. (page 126)

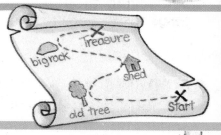

route A way to go from one place to another. Follow the **route** on the map to find the treasure. (page 30)

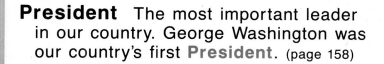

rule Rules tell us what to do and what not to do. This swim club has **rules**. (page 48)

services Jobs that workers do for others. Doctors do **services** for others. (page 88)

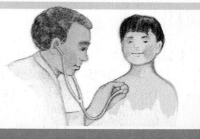

settlement A small community built by settlers. The settlers built the houses of their settlement. (page 149)

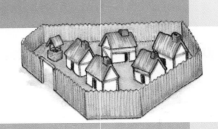

settler A person who comes from another country to live in a new country. Many settlers came to America by boat. (page 148)

state Part of a country. I live in the state of Kansas. (page 5)

suburb A community just outside of a city. We live in a suburb of a very big city. (page 24)

symbol Something that stands for something else. These symbols stand for a tree, a tent, and a river. (page 3)

Tree
Tent
River

tax Money that people pay to their community. We pay tax money to the community for services. (page 90)

Pay Taxes Here

time line A time line shows the order in which things happened. This time line shows some of the things Amy did in one day. (page 190)

morning | afternoon | evening

town A small community. This town has hills around it. (page 25)

transportation A way of moving people from place to place. The train is my favorite kind of transportation. (page 26)

valley Low land between hills or mountains. This valley has many flowers in the summer. (page 124)

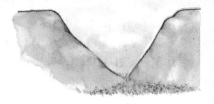

village A community that is smaller than a town. This Indian village has a tall fence around it. (page 145)

volunteer A service worker who works without pay. This volunteer is selling food for the museum. (page 92)

vote To choose something. We vote to go to the park. (page 56)

wants Things we would like to have but can live without. This jump rope and bike are wants. (page 71)

White House Where the President of the United States lives and works. The White House is in Washington, D.C. (page 173)

INDEX

CREDITS